— What are you doing? I'm arresting you for doing molka.
— You're wrong. I'm just keeping my eye on a criminal suspect, and she was taking a shower by coincidence.
— What did she do wrong?
— Last night, I saw her running a red light at an intersection.

I have a hunch that somebody is watching me whenever I take a shower. I'd better move to another city for my safety.

I was lucky I could get this job as a garbageman—all because local people truly hate 3-D jobs. I'm now working happily with a relatively higher wage, and I can commute to work in my BMW sedan.

I'm now wrestling with my computer in the office all day long, while just earning minimum wage. But my personal vanity won't allow me to work on a 3-D job. I'm happily commuting with my bicycle, and on the positive side, it makes me stronger.

I know his remarks are nothing but sour grapes.

I'm only motivated by money, and I'm running to achieve the world record for the 100-meter race because NIKE promised me billions of dollars as a bonus. With that money, I'll be able to retire ASAP and lead a cozy lifestyle for the rest of my life.

I'm able to run faster than both of them. I don't understand why NIKE hasn't tried to scout me. If they continue to ignore me, I will meet Adidas or Reebok next month.

I'm self-motivated. I'm not running to make money, and I am determined to run until my last days. I just love running.

We're making a living now by taking bribes from the gangsters because the government can't afford to pay us anymore. No business, except the drug cartels, has survived due to the rampant crimes. We admit there's a symbiosis between the gangs and us.

We're making a living by selling drugs to the police. They're big customers for us.

In this crime-ridden country, we have no choice but to join the Mafia and live as their soldiers. Every job has evaporated because of the war between law enforcement officers and the drug cartels.

OPEN TO DEBATE 1
30 KOREAN ISSUES
WRITTEN BY LIS KOREA EDITORIAL STAFF & NEAL D. WILLIAMS

LIS KOREA

Major New Edition

Introduction

This discussion book has been written for English language students who wish to study and discuss contemporary Korean issues in English. The book considers a wide range of issues, from *drinking culture* to *TV dramas*, from *COVID-19* to *LGBTQ*, from *low birth rate* to *planning for retirement*. Each lesson is introduced with a topic preview, consisting of several thought-provoking questions. The preview is followed by an authentic model conversation in which two individuals discuss an aspect of the issue being considered in the unit. These conversations use idiomatic language, the same type of language that native speakers of English use in normal dialogue. Next, there is a reading passage that provides an overview of the main ideas related to the issue. Every attempt has been made to use the most current information, statistics, and perspectives in the reading section. Please note that all of the stories in the reading passages are true, and the individuals mentioned are real people. Key words and expressions are highlighted in the reading passage.

Following the reading passage, the key words and expressions are defined in easy-to-understand language. Each key word or expression is then used in a sentence in order to illustrate the meaning in context. As every student of the English language knows, an individual word can have numerous meanings, and common words can have uncommon meanings. Therefore, each word or expression that is defined in this book is given the proper definition that fits with the context of the reading passage. For example, one common meaning of the word *bound* is "tied up." However, *bound* can also mean "sure, certain, destined." The latter definition is the only one that applies to the reading passage in this book, so that is the only definition that is cited.

After key words and expressions are defined, readers are given seven questions designed to provoke discussion. These questions are almost all questions of opinion, not questions of fact. In other words, students should feel free to express their own opinion since there is no right or wrong answer to the questions. Some of the questions are simply fascinating quotes that can be used as a basis for discussion.

Finally, as an added bonus, each unit concludes with a "current hot topic." There is a short reading passage about a controversial aspect of the topic being considered in the unit, along with two discussion questions.

For matters of style, this book mostly follows *The Chicago Manual of Style*.

Dedication

This book is dedicated to my lovely wife and best friend, *Eunkyung Won*.

Suggestions to the Student

Carnegie Hall in New York City was opened in 1891 and is now one of the world's most famous concert halls. Every musician dreams of performing there at some point in their career. An old joke asks the question: "How do you get to Carnegie Hall?" The answer: "Practice, practice, practice!" Many students of the English language frequently ask their teacher a similar question: "How can I become a great English speaker?" The best answer is: "Speak, speak, speak!" Of course, you have to know some grammar and vocabulary, but once you have a reasonable knowledge of those aspects, your skill in speaking English will depend on how much time you spend actually using the language.

Studies have shown that English speakers can become fairly fluent in Spanish with about 600 hours of practice. The same is true of Spanish speakers who want to learn English. The amount of time needed is fairly low because English and Spanish are somewhat similar. However, if an English speaker wants to learn Korean, that learner will need to invest about 2,200 hours of practice in using the language, and the same is true for a Korean speaker who wants to learn English. The two languages are dramatically different in appearance, grammar, and pronunciation, so much more time is needed. If you want to become a skillful English speaker, you need to accumulate as much time as possible in actually speaking the language.

One easy way to build up time in speaking English is to enroll in an English conversation class. When you are in your class, you should speak as much as you can. It is important that you do not worry about using the correct grammar; just keep speaking, and you will communicate. You will also, slowly but surely, improve your conversational skills. The English learners who have become fluent in English are no smarter than you. They just kept trying to use English and speaking as much as possible until they gained some level of fluency. You can do the same!

Suggestions to the Teacher

If you are an English language teacher, you are naturally interested in inspiring your students to speak English as much as possible. How can this goal be accomplished? Here are several practical suggestions. First, it is important to emphasize to students that the discussion questions written in this book simply provide an opportunity to express one's opinion. There is no right or wrong answer. Language experts say that one of the most important duties of a language teacher is to reduce anxiety in the classroom. Therefore, it is crucial to convince students that everyone's opinion is valid and important.

Second, because the aim of a language course is to get students involved in speaking the language as much as possible, it is better to use pair work than group discussions. When students are in groups, they may feel intimidated by more fluent speakers, and they will feel reluctant to speak. However, if they are working in pairs, they are conversing with a partner and have no choice but to speak. As they speak more with their partner, they will gain in confidence and fluency.

Third, teachers need to emphasize to students that simply *trying* to speak in English will help them achieve their goal of fluency. Of course, students will often experience some stress when trying to express their opinion in another language. They may feel as though their grammar and vocabulary are inadequate and that they should speak using only grammar that is completely accurate. Effective teachers will explain to students that it's necessary to feel some stress, but that's not anything to worry about. Students should just keep talking, using the vocabulary and grammar that they already know. Over time, they will improve in speaking, as well as in vocabulary and grammar.

Open to Debate (1): 30 Korean Issues

Table of Contents

Introduction 06

Suggestions to the Student 07

Suggestions to the Teacher 08

Issue 01	BTS 10	Issue 16	Planning for Retirement 70
Issue 02	Corruption and Transparency 14	Issue 17	Plastic Surgery 74
Issue 03	COVID-19 18	Issue 18	Rising Crime Rate 78
Issue 04	Digital Sex Crimes 22	Issue 19	Rising Obesity 82
Issue 05	Divorce 26	Issue 20	Scams and More Scams 86
Issue 06	Dog Meat 30	Issue 21	Sexual Harassment 90
Issue 07	Drinking Culture 34	Issue 22	Smartphone Addiction 94
Issue 08	Health Supplements 38	Issue 23	Suicide 98
Issue 09	High Cost of Dying 42	Issue 24	Tattoo Artistry 102
Issue 10	Housing Bubble 46	Issue 25	The Republic of Seoul 106
Issue 11	International Workers 50	Issue 26	Too Much Work 110
Issue 12	LGBTQ 54	Issue 27	Traffic Accidents 114
Issue 13	Low Birth Rate 58	Issue 28	TV Dramas 118
Issue 14	North Korea, China, and Japan 62	Issue 29	Value of a College Education 122
Issue 15	Obsession with Sports 66	Issue 30	Where to Invest 126

Appendix: Notes about Grammar and Style 130

Discussion Textbooks from LIS KOREA 132

BTS IS SAID TO BE A REINCARNATION OF THE BEATLES. DO YOU THINK SO?

We're the king of boy bands ON EARTH. Our popularity will continue for a long time, and no band will compete with us in the near future.

We're the best band IN HEAVEN. But sometimes we long for the day when we could play ON EARTH once again. Be sure to know that your popularity can go up in smoke in an instant.

Topic Preview:

What do you know about the Korean boy band BTS? Do you own any of their CDs? What are your favorite songs that they sing? Why do some people call BTS "the most popular boy band in the world"?

Dialogue:

Jack: Nora, have you been to any concerts lately?

Nora: No, I haven't, actually. I don't go to concerts that often. The last one I went to was in 2018.

Jack: Oh really? What singer or group did you go to see?

Nora: I went to see BTS. They performed at the Staples Center in LA for four nights in September 2018.

Jack: Wow! You saw BTS in person? Lucky you!

Nora: Yes, I was lucky. I have a cousin who lives in LA, and she got tickets for us both.

Jack: Nice! What were your favorite songs at that concert?

Nora: Oh, all the songs were great, but I especially liked "Idol," "Save Me," "DNA," "Fake Love," and "Mic Drop."

Jack: Those are all great. By the way, I heard that BTS was taking a break, so each member could do his own solo work.

Nora: I heard that too. I hope that they don't break up. That would be a tragedy.

Jack: Yeah, I agree. They have millions of fans around the world.

Time magazine debuted in 1923, and for a century, it has been one of the most circulated magazines in the United States. *Time* set out to tell the news by emphasizing the most influential people of the day. Appearing on the cover of *Time* has become an indicator of a subject's celebrity status, eminence, or notoriety. In 2018, many readers were surprised to see a Korean boy band named BTS on the cover of the October 18th issue of *Time*. The caption read "Next Generation Leaders." How did BTS become significant enough to grace the cover of *Time*?

BTS consists of seven members: Jin, Suga, J-Hope, RM, Jimin, V, and Jungkook. The group debuted in South Korea in 2013, with the single album *2 Cool 4 Skool*. In 2014, the group released their first Korean-language studio album, *Dark & Wild*, as well as a Japanese-language studio album, *Wake Up*. By 2017, BTS entered the global music market, breaking numerous sales records. BTS became one of the few groups since the Beatles to have four US number one albums in less than two years. The group's many accolades include nine American Music Awards, 12 Billboard Music Awards, 24 Golden Disk Awards, and nominations for two Grammy Awards. They have partnered with UNICEF and spoken to the United Nations. In 2019, they even appeared on *Time*'s list of the 100 most influential people in the world.

The question remains: how did a Korean boy band gain such worldwide popularity? According to BTS fans, the group's phenomenal success is due to its authenticity, chemistry, and teamwork. Also, the themes of their songs are practical, timely, and meaningful. Many of their songs are based on love, relationships, loving ourselves, reality, and mental health. In short, they are making music that people want to listen to.

ISSUE 01 BTS

Vocabulary & Expressions:

debut
*to make a first appearance or entrance into society
- The famous Hershey Chocolate Bar *debuted* on November 11, 1900.

circulated
*sold or distributed, especially over a wide area
- *What's Cooking* is the most *circulated* magazine in Canada.

set out
*to begin with a definite purpose; to intend, undertake
- Johnny Depp *set out* to become a musician, but he ended up becoming an actor.

subject
*the person or thing discussed; the topic
- The president's personal life has been the *subject* of many rumors.

eminence
*the condition of being well known and respected. Not to be confused with *imminence*, which refers to something that is soon to occur.
- After Arnold Schwarzenegger gained *eminence* as an actor, he entered politics and became governor of California.

notoriety
*the condition of being widely known for some bad characteristic
- Politicians convicted of crimes gain *notoriety* and are rarely elected again.

grace
*to make something more attractive; to adorn, enhance
- The halls of the expensive house were *graced* with many fine paintings.

accolade
*any award, honor, or expression of praise
- The 1997 film *Titanic* received numerous *accolades*, including eleven Academy Awards.

phenomenal
*very remarkable, extraordinary
- My father has a *phenomenal* memory; he never forgets anything.

authenticity
*a quality of genuineness, representing one's true nature and sincere character
- Soban Restaurant in LA is known for its *authenticity*; it represents the best of traditional Korean food.

chemistry
*a sense of harmony shown when people work together effectively
- CEOs try to form work teams that have good *chemistry*, so they can work together well.

meaningful
*full of meaning, significance, purpose, or value
- *The Bucket List* (2007) is one of the most *meaningful* films I have ever seen; it really made me think about life.

Open to Debate (1): *30 Korean Issues*

Discussion Points:

1. Why do you think BTS became the most popular boy band in the world?
2. Do you think BTS has enhanced the reputation of Korea around the world? In what ways?
3. BTS has been nominated twice for a Grammy Award. Why do you think they didn't win?
4. Most boy bands have a short life span. How long do you think BTS will be popular? Will they still be performing 10 years from now?
5. In June 2022, BTS announced that they were taking a break from group performances in order to focus on solo projects. Do you think this announcement means that they will break up?
6. Some music critics accuse boy bands of emphasizing the appearance and marketing of the group more than the quality and originality of their music. Do you think BTS is guilty of this criticism?
7. Do you have a favorite BTS member? Why do you like him?

Current Hot Topic: Korean Movies Win International Acclaim

The Academy of Motion Picture Arts and Sciences presents awards for artistic merit in the film industry. The awards are called the "Academy Awards" or the "Oscars." Something amazing happened at the 92nd Academy Awards, held in Hollywood on February 9, 2020. A South Korean film, *Parasite*, directed by Bong Joon-ho, won four awards: Best Picture, Best Director, Best Original Screenplay, and Best International Feature Film. *Parasite* was the first non-English language film in Academy Awards history to win Best Picture. Korean artistry was recognized again in 2021, when Youn Yuh-jung won Best Supporting Actress for her role in *Minari*.

For Further Discussion:

1. The main themes of *Parasite* are class conflict, social inequality, and wealth disparity. Do you think these themes reflect real life in South Korea today? In what ways?
2. Have you seen the film *Parasite*? What were the most memorable scenes, in your opinion?

It's useless to be angry about shady officials. They enjoy lots of give-and-take relationships with powerful people. They will never budge on the corruption issue.

Your indifferent attitude just provides them with breeding grounds for corruption to grow. You're an accomplice to corruption!

Corrupt officials should be held accountable! I'm determined to root out corruption in our government!

— I don't understand why they're angry about our relationship.
— They're the ones who should pay for the price of our friendship. You don't have to worry, however. We know how to make their anger subside. We'll increase the minimum wage by 10 percent next year.

Topic Preview:

Where would you rank your country's level of corruption, using a scale of 0 (highly corrupt) to 100 (very clean)? Have you ever checked your country's level of corruption on the "Corruption Perceptions Index," published each year by Transparency.org? What countries do you think are the least corrupt in the world? What countries are the most corrupt? What is the best way to eliminate corruption in your country?

Dialogue:

Henry: Hey, Grace. Have you seen the latest corruption index from Transparency.org?

Grace: No, I haven't. I wonder how my home country of New Zealand was ranked.

Henry: You're kidding, right? You must know that New Zealand is always one of the *least* corrupt countries in the world.

Grace: Well, I know that they don't have much corruption, but I don't know their exact ranking.

Henry: I'm sure they're among the top three least corrupt countries.

Grace: Okay. That's good to hear.

Henry: Why do you think New Zealand has very little corruption?

Grace: I think it's because we have two very competent law enforcement agencies: the Serious Fraud Office and the Independent Police Conduct Authority.

Henry: Well, that's great that they take their jobs so seriously.

Grace: By the way, how did the United States rank in the latest transparency index?

Henry: As an American, I am too embarrassed to say.

Corruption and Transparency

Corruption in government is a familiar theme in recent Korean history. When Roh Moo-hyun ran for president of the Republic of Korea, he promised to "clean up the presidency" and "root out corruption." In his inaugural speech in 2003, Roh promised that his administration would be built on "principle and trust, transparency, and fairness." He stated that "corruption must be eliminated not only for the continued growth of the economy but also for the health of society." After Roh left office, allegations of corruption arose regarding his family and aides, some of whom were indicted on charges of taking bribes. In response, Roh committed suicide in 2009.

When Lee Myung-bak became president in 2008, he said, "These are my promises to you: I will serve the people and bring peace to this nation." He promised that "the government will do its best, to act with integrity." In 2018, five years after Lee left office, he was arrested on charges of bribery, embezzlement, and tax evasion, which occurred during his presidency. Prosecutors accused Lee of receiving bribes totaling 11 billion won and moving assets of 35 billion won to an illegal slush fund. Lee was convicted and sentenced to 17 years in prison.

When Park Geun-hye became president in 2013, she said in her inaugural speech, "I will earn the trust of the people by ensuring that our government remains clean, transparent, and competent. I will try to shed popular distrust of government." In 2017, while still in office, Park was arrested and charged with abuse of power, bribery, coercion, and leaking government secrets. She denied the charges but was sentenced to 24 years in prison. She was later pardoned by President Moon Jae-in because of her failing health and the need to promote national unity.

ISSUE 02 — CORRUPTION AND TRANSPARENCY

Vocabulary & Expressions:

root out
*to find and remove something or someone
- The high school principal was determined to *root out* cheating in the school.

corruption
*dishonest or illegal behavior
- Denmark is well known for honesty in government and business; there is very little *corruption*.

inaugural
*relating to the ceremony of introducing a person into office
- President Obama delivered his *inaugural* address on January 21, 2009.

transparency
*the operation of a government or organization in a clear, accountable, and truthful manner
- When governments practice *transparency*, it's easy for citizens to see exactly how their government operates.

indict
*to formally charge someone with a crime
- Actor Robert Downey Jr. has been *indicted* several times for possession of illegal drugs.

bribe
*something given to a person in order to influence a decision or action in a dishonest manner
- A *bribe* most often consists of money, but it could be anything of value.

integrity
*total honesty and sincerity
- People with *integrity* do what is right, not what is easy or popular.

embezzlement
*the stealing of money or property entrusted to one's care
- The secretary was guilty of *embezzlement* of $10,000 from the company bank account.

tax evasion
*a crime that occurs when someone avoids or refuses to pay their taxes
- Actor Wesley Snipes was convicted of *tax evasion* and sentenced to three years in prison.

slush fund
*a secret fund of money used for illegal or corrupt political purposes, such as bribery
- President Richard Nixon's presidential campaign used a *slush fund* to try to silence the Watergate criminals.

shed
*to get rid of; to eliminate
- I think I need to *shed* a few kilograms of weight.

coercion
*the use of force or threat to cause another person to do what you want
- The school bully used *coercion* to get another boy's lunch money.

pardon
*to free someone from the penalty of a crime
- During his eight years in office, President Barack Obama *pardoned* more than 200 individuals who had been convicted of federal crimes.

Open to Debate (1): 30 Korean Issues

Discussion Points:

1. Why is it so difficult for Korean presidents to eliminate corruption?
2. Do you think the prison sentences given to presidents Lee and Park were appropriate?
3. Do you agree with the decision to pardon former president Park?
4. Which president in your country has been the least corrupt, in your opinion?

Read the following quotes about corruption.
Can you explain what they mean? Do you agree with the idea expressed?

5. Power tends to corrupt, and absolute power corrupts absolutely. Great men are almost always bad men. Lord Acton
6. Corruption is the price we pay for democracy. Unknown
7. Politics doesn't corrupt people; people corrupt politics. Amit Kalantri

Current Hot Topic: Special Privileges for Children of the Elite

When Moon Jae-in became president of South Korea in 2017, he pledged that he would build a nation free of special privileges and injustice. After several years of his presidency, some Koreans began to doubt that basic rules of fairness were being followed. Cho Kuk, minister of justice, was accused of falsifying the academic achievements of his daughter, Cho Min, and helping her gain unfair admission into Korea University and Busan University Medical School. President Moon later appointed Choo Mi-ae as minister of justice. She too was accused of obtaining special privileges for her son during his military service.

For Further Discussion:

1. Can you cite any other examples of special privileges that have been given to children of government or business leaders?
2. During your years in education, have you personally seen examples of special treatment for the elite or the wealthy? What happened?

— What are you doing?
— I'm readying myself to fight off the coronavirus.
— With your shield and sword?
— Absolutely!
— Why don't you wear a mask first? I'm afraid you'll lose the war with the virus without a mask.
— No, I won't wear it! I can't get enough oxygen to fight while wearing a mask on my face.

Topic Preview:

How has the COVID-19 pandemic affected you and your family? What measures did you take to protect yourself against the coronavirus? Have you been satisfied with your government's response to the pandemic? What changes need to be made for your country to get back to normal?

Dialogue:

Lucas: Mia, you won't believe what I saw yesterday!

Mia: What are you talking about?

Lucas: My sister and I went to a local museum, and we saw a big argument about mask requirements.

Mia: Oh, wow! What happened?

Lucas: Well, some places have stopped mask requirements, but some businesses, like this museum, still require them.

Mia: And someone refused to wear one?

Lucas: Yeah, there was this middle-aged man who kept arguing that masks should no longer be required because the pandemic is going away.

Mia: Oh, that's ridiculous! It's such a simple thing to wear a mask to protect yourself and others against COVID-19.

Lucas: Of course, I agree. Well, this guy kept refusing, so the museum called the police, and he was escorted out.

Mia: It's too bad that we don't have a mask-wearing culture like many Asian counties.

Lucas: You can say that again.

COVID-19

In 1996, an American English teacher came to South Korea to teach English. Like all expats, he experienced some episodes of culture shock. He found some aspects of Korean culture to be off-putting, such as having to share side dishes with others. Other Korean customs were simply amusing. For example, he wondered why he frequently saw Koreans wearing a mask in public. In the US, if you saw someone wearing a mask in a public place, you would assume that the person had just had dental surgery. Koreans apparently wore a mask simply because they had a cold. In due time, the American teacher realized that Koreans who wore a mask did so as an act of kindness, with the purpose of shielding other people from catching their cold.

Years later, when the coronavirus emerged in early 2020, causing the COVID-19 pandemic, the Korean conscientious habit of wearing a mask proved to be a valuable tool in fighting the spread of COVID-19. When the coronavirus first appeared, no one could have predicted the death and havoc that would ensue. Just two years later, in early 2022, the death toll topped six million people worldwide. Some countries handled the disease more effectively than others. After two years of the pandemic, the death rate per one million people in the US and Brazil topped 3,100, and in France, Italy, the UK, and Russia, the death toll was more than 2,000. Meanwhile, the death rate per one million people was 478 in South Korea and 291 in Taiwan. One of the major reasons that the rate was so low in those Asian countries was because they have a strong tradition of wearing masks. While many Americans ranted against mask mandates, Koreans were quietly wearing their masks and protecting their fellow citizens.

ISSUE 03 COVID-19

Vocabulary & Expressions:

expat *an *expatriate*, meaning a person who leaves his/her home country to live and work in another country. Not to be confused with *ex-patriot*, which refers to someone who is no longer loyal to his home country.
- Among the two million *expats* living in Korea are thousands of English teachers.

off-putting *causing dislike, uneasiness, annoyance, or repulsion
- My cousin invited me to watch a horror movie; it was such an *off-putting* film that I walked out.

in due time *eventually; at an appropriate time
- When we asked our teacher for tips about the exam, she said she would give us more information *in due time*.

shield *to protect or hide someone or something from danger or harm
- When the sun is bright, you should always wear sunglasses to *shield* your eyes from the sun.

emerge *to become known; to come into view or notice
- Arizona's Zac Gallen has *emerged* as one of Major League Baseball's best pitchers.

pandemic *an outbreak of a disease that occurs over a wide geographic area and affects many people
- An *epidemic* is a disease that affects many people in a community, region, or country; a *pandemic* is an epidemic that spreads across multiple countries.

conscientious *describing a person who is always careful to do what is right
- My father was a very *conscientious* worker; he was never late for work.

prove to be *to turn out to be
- Some workers didn't like the new manager at first, but he *proved to be* an excellent boss.

havoc *damage, destruction, or devastation
- The hurricane caused great *havoc* in many cities.

ensue *to follow as a result of some event
- After the team won the World Cup, a great celebration *ensued*.

rant *to talk loudly and excitedly
- My uncle is always *ranting* against the new president.

mandate *a command or instruction from someone in authority
- Because of COVID-19, the US government issued a mask *mandate*, requiring all passengers on airplanes to wear a mask.

● ● ● ● *Open to Debate (1): 30 Korean Issues*

● *Discussion Points:*

1. What other factors, besides mask wearing, helped Koreans to handle the COVID-19 pandemic in such an effective manner?
2. Have you, or someone you know, ever gotten COVID-19? What were the symptoms?
3. Do you know anyone who died from COVID-19? What happened?
4. Have you heard about any celebrities or politicians who got COVID-19? What happened?
5. Some Americans refused to wear a mask during the pandemic and were even arrested. Did you ever hear about such incidents in your country?
6. Nowadays, do you always wear a mask when you go out? Under what circumstances do you not wear a mask?
7. Besides wearing a mask, what other steps have you taken to protect yourself against COVID-19? Have you been vaccinated?
8. Do you think everyone should be required to get the COVID-19 vaccination? Why or why not?

● *Current Hot Topic:* **COVID-19 and Korean Business**

The COVID-19 pandemic brought havoc to businesses around the world, including Korea. Public bathhouses and saunas are a vital part of traditional Korean culture. However, due to the difficulties of maintaining social distancing between customers, the government forced such "high-risk facilities" to close. Some of them will never reopen. The film industry was also hurt by the pandemic. In contrast, Korean exports of semiconductors, electric vehicles, and medical supplies, such as masks, gloves, and sanitizers, increased dramatically. Meanwhile, with concert venues closed, K-pop artists turned to virtual concerts. BTS set the record for the most watched virtual concerts in 2020.

● *For Further Discussion:*

1. How has the COVID pandemic affected other Korean businesses and institutions? How did schools and universities change their operation?
2. During the pandemic, did you order more products online? What kind of products?

— What are you doing? I'm arresting you for doing molka.
— You're wrong. I'm just keeping my eye on a criminal suspect, and she was taking a shower by coincidence.
— What did she do wrong?
— Last night, I saw her running a red light at an intersection.

I have a hunch that somebody is watching me whenever I take a shower. I'd better move to another city for my safety.

Topic Preview:

How often do you chat online? What types of software for chatting have you used? Have you, or someone you know, ever been sexually harassed online? What happened? Do you think the punishment for digital sex crimes in your country is strong enough?

Dialogue:

Sophia: Mason, do you have Netflix?

Mason: Yes, I do, actually. Don't you have it?

Sophia: No, I don't at the moment, but I'm thinking about subscribing. Is it really worth the cost?

Mason: Yes, I think so. I have seen so many great TV shows on Netflix, including many Korean dramas, such as *Squid Game*, *Kingdom*, *Mr. Sunshine*, and *Itaewon Class*.

Sophia: Well, those dramas sound really interesting. Does Netflix have many documentaries?

Mason: Yes, of course. I just recently watched one called *Cyber Hell: Exposing an Internet Horror*.

Sophia: That sounds interesting. What is it about?

Mason: It's about how some sexual predators were caught after they had harassed young girls online.

Sophia: Oh, my! That sounds awful, but I think I'd like to see how those criminals were captured.

Mason: Well, if you like, you can watch the documentary at my place. It's less than two hours long.

Sophia: That sounds great, thanks! How about Friday night?

Mason: Okay. Sounds good. I'll invite a few more friends over too.

Digital Sex Crimes

In 2019, a young Korean girl was chatting online, when a man using the online moniker "Baksa" asked her about modeling. He said he was a talent scout for a clothing company and was looking for new models. She expressed interest, so he asked her for a few pictures of her face and full-length shots. Then he persuaded her to take a few pictures in her underwear. He praised her good looks and said she would make a great model. He just needed the information from her national ID card in order to process payments. After getting her personal information, he demanded more revealing shots, including nude pictures. He threatened to send the risqué pictures he had already taken to her family and friends. She reluctantly agreed.

For two years, Baksa used this modus operandi to coerce 25 victims into sending him sexually explicit content. He then made the illicit images available to online viewers, who had to pay a fee, using cryptocurrency. Eventually, a thorough investigation conducted by Korean police led to the discovery of Baksa's identity. He was 25-year-old Cho Ju-bin, who was subsequently convicted and sent to prison for 40 years. Meanwhile, another online predator, using the ID "Godgod," acquired 20 online victims through a series of crimes that became known as the "Nth Room Case." He was revealed to be Moon Hyeong-wook, and he was sentenced to 34 years in prison. Investigations in these cases led to almost 4,000 arrests, with hundreds of individuals sent to prison. The chat rooms were shut down, but the illegal images are still being disseminated globally on the dark web.

These sex crimes only added to South Korea's epidemic of what is called *molka*, a Korean word for the online distribution of nonconsensual sex videos taken of women.

ISSUE 04 DIGITAL SEX CRIMES

Vocabulary & Expressions:

moniker — *a nickname; an online ID used to hide a person's true identity
- Keanu Reeves was such an outstanding hockey goalie that his college teammates gave him the *moniker* "The Wall."

talent scout — *a person who finds individuals with talent for a specific field or activity
- In 2006, a *talent scout* discovered a talented singer named Stefani Germanotta, who later became known as Lady Gaga.

revealing — *showing more of a person's body than is usual for the situation
- *Revealing* clothing is okay for the beach but not for the office.

risqué — *describing language, actions, or appearances that seem indecent, improper, or offensive
- Smart workers avoid telling *risqué* jokes that will offend others.

modus operandi — *a person's usual way of doing something; abbreviated as M.O.
- Most criminals have a *modus operandi* that they follow in almost every crime.

explicit — *clear and open in showing nudity or sexuality
- *Explicit* books and films are banned in many countries because their content is considered offensive.

illicit — *not permitted; illegal or unlawful
- People who post *illicit* images online can be arrested.

cryptocurrency — *a digital form of money produced by a public network (instead of a government) that uses cryptography (special computer codes) to keep payments secret and secure
- Bitcoin was the first *cryptocurrency* to be introduced, in 2009.

predator — *one who injures, uses, or exploits others for personal gain or profit
- Parents should download special software, like Net Nanny or SafeToNet, to protect their kids from online *predators*.

disseminate — *to scatter or spread widely
- News of the politician's scandal was *disseminated* widely on the Internet.

dark web — *a secret, encrypted part of the Internet that is only accessible with special web browsers, such as Tor (The Onion Router)
- The *surface web* includes sites available to anyone, like Google and Wikipedia; the *deep web* includes sites that require a password, like an online bank account; the *dark web* includes sites that support illegal activities, such as selling drugs.

nonconsensual — *not agreed to by one or more of the people involved
- *Nonconsensual* sex is illegal in every country in the world.

Open to Debate (1): 30 Korean Issues

Open to Debate (1): 30 Korean Issues

Discussion Points:

1. What are the best ways to stop online sexual predators like Cho and Moon?
2. Why would a teenager agree to send explicit photos to a stranger online in the hopes of a modeling career?
3. Cho and Moon used an instant messaging service called Telegram, which provides encrypted chats. Such services as Telegram and Wickr allow participants to hide illegal images. Do you think these services should be prohibited?
4. Some people say that all online chatters and posters should be required to prove their real identity before being allowed to use online platforms. Do you agree with this idea?
5. Cryptocurrency is often used to hide crimes. Do you think cryptocurrency should be banned altogether for this reason?
6. According to recent studies, one out of five minors in Seoul is at risk of falling victim to an online sex crime. Why do you think this crime is so widespread?
7. In 2022, the investigation described in the reading passage was made into a Netflix documentary called *Cyber Hell: Exposing an Internet Horror*. Would you be interested in watching it?

Current Hot Topic: Punishment for Sex Crimes

In 2008, a man named Cho Doo-soon brutally raped an eight-year-old girl in Ansan, Gyeonggi. The girl survived, but 80% of her lower organs were completely dysfunctional. Because of Cho's 18 prior criminal convictions, prosecutors asked for a life sentence. Instead, the court sentenced him to only 12 years in prison, accepting Cho's argument that he was too drunk to remember anything. Because of Cho's case, some laws were strengthened. However, in 2019, well-known entertainers Jung Joon-young and Choi Jong-hoon were found guilty of gang rape and illicit filming and sharing. They received only a five-year prison sentence.

For Further Discussion:

1. Should a criminal's sentence be reduced because he was drunk or on drugs?
2. How many years in prison should Cho have received for his crimes? What about Jung and Choi?

— Wow! You have three grand houses. I guess you've made lots of money. What's your job?
— I'm just a housekeeper, but a marvelous one.
— Why do you call yourself a "marvelous housekeeper"?
— Every time I left a man, I kept his house.
— Oh, really? Are you considering a fourth marriage?
— Not until one of my houses is sold. I can't manage more than three houses at the same time.

She's a first-rate housekeeper but not a good animal keeper. She's too busy managing three houses to take care of me. I don't understand why my dad left me with her.

Topic Preview:

Do you have any friends whose parents have divorced? How often do they talk about it? Can you think of any celebrities who got divorced? Do you know what their reasons were? What do you think are acceptable reasons for divorce?

Dialogue:

Liam: Ava, I just got some bad news.

Ava: Oh, Liam, I'm sorry to hear that. What kind of bad news?

Liam: My parents are getting a divorce.

Ava: Oh, that's sad to hear. Do you know why they're choosing divorce?

Liam: Well, I don't think cheating was involved. I think they just drifted apart.

Ava: How long have they been married?

Liam: They've been together 26 years.

Ava: Wow! That's a long time.

Liam: Yeah, my sister and I knew that neither of them has been happy in the marriage for a long time.

Ava: Well, you are both adults, so you are mature enough to handle the situation.

Liam: Yeah, I guess you're right.

Ava: Yeah, divorce is sad, but when unhappy people stay together, the situation can get worse.

Koreans were once proud of the fact that they had one of the lowest divorce rates in the world. However, in the 1970s, the divorce rate began to rise. It picked up momentum in the early 1990s. In fact, the divorce rate more than quadrupled between 1990 and 2017. As women gained more financial freedom and independence, they began to realize that they no longer had to follow the old adage to "endure, endure, endure" a bad marriage.

In recent years, even many older Koreans who have been together for 25 or 30 years are calling it quits. Such divorces are often called "gray divorces" or "twilight divorces." One reason for this trend may be found in the fact that Koreans' life expectancy has surged dramatically in the past few decades. One study ranked Korea in third place for life expectancy, exceeded only by Japan and Singapore. Korean men can now expect to live to 80.5 years and Korean women to 86.5 years. With the expectation of such a long life, many older Koreans no longer feel compelled to tolerate an unhappy marriage.

In previous generations, the subject of divorce was a taboo topic for conversation. However, that old custom has recently given way to openness to discuss this new reality. In late 2020, TV Chosun launched a new reality show entitled *We Got Divorced*. The show features divorced couples ranging in age from their 20s to those in their 70s. While the show faced some criticism, it was ranked No. 4 on Netflix Korea. Another show, SBS's *My Ugly Duckling*, featured four divorced men: comedian Kim Jun-ho, rapper Lee Sang-min, singer Tak Jae-hoon, and actor Im Won-hee. They engaged in a lighthearted discussion about how to deal with divorce, and they avoided portraying divorce as a moral failure.

ISSUE 05 DIVORCE

Vocabulary & Expressions:

pick up
*to increase
- After the bus driver got outside the city, he **picked up** speed on the open highway.

momentum
*strength or force gained by movement or by a series of events
- Smith's presidential campaign increased **momentum** after he promised to lower taxes.

quadruple
*to make or become four times as great or as many
- Because of the company's success, the CEO **quadrupled** the number of workers.

adage
*an old familiar saying; a proverb
- My father used to quote an old **adage**: "Early to bed and early to rise, makes a man healthy, wealthy, and wise."

call it quits
*to quit; to stop working, abandon something, give up; to end a situation or relationship
- After working hard for forty years, my father **called it quits** and finally retired.

twilight
*a period in which one's life, strength, importance, or power are declining
- My grandparents bought a nice retirement home near the beach, where they can enjoy their **twilight** years.

surge
*to rise suddenly and greatly
- Due to inflation, the price of everything has **surged** recently.

compelled
*to do something because of physical, moral, mental, or social pressure
- Everyone in my group made a donation to the local charity, so I felt **compelled** to donate something too.

tolerate
*to endure a situation; to put up with an unpleasant person or situation
- My boss was so unpleasant that I could not **tolerate** him any longer, and I quit my job.

taboo
*banned by society as improper, offensive, or unacceptable
- There are some **taboo** words that you cannot say on TV.

give way to
*to be replaced by
- It's sad when local farmland **gives way to** shopping malls.

lighthearted
*free from care, worry, or seriousness
- My mom is easy to talk to; she is always in a **lighthearted** mood.

● ● ● ● Open to Debate (1): *30 Korean Issues*

Discussion Points:

1. What do you think are the main reasons that the divorce rate has increased in Korea?
2. Why are so many older Korean couples getting divorced?
3. Koreans used to think of divorce as a moral failure. Do you think that view is still common?
4. Do you know anyone who has gotten a divorce? What is their life like?

Read the following quotes about divorce.
Can you explain what they mean? Do you agree with the idea expressed?

5. The way I look at it, if you want the rainbow, you've got to put up with the rain. Dolly Parton
6. When people divorce, it's always such a tragedy. At the same time, if people stay together, it can be even worse. Monica Bellucci
7. Sometimes good things fall apart, so better things can fall together. Marilyn Monroe

Current Hot Topic: A Crusade against "Bad Fathers"

Divorce is especially sad when children are involved. Unfortunately, some divorced parents, especially fathers, refuse to pay child support. One study revealed that 80% of single Korean parents were not receiving child support payments from the other parent, and 72% had never received any payment at all. Koo Bon-chang, a 59-year-old retiree, has begun a one-man crusade to humiliate such "bad fathers" by exposing their failure to pay child support on his website, along with their photos and personal information. He has been sued almost 30 times, investigated by the police, and fined. He has vowed to continue his fight.

For Further Discussion:

1. Why do so many fathers refuse to pay child support? Is it acceptable for the government to take away a father's driver's license until he pays his child support?
2. Do you think Koo Bon-chang's one-man crusade is a good idea? Will it be effective?

— Hey Charlie. Have you seen Max lately? He seems to have just disappeared.
— No, Buddy, I haven't seen Max in over a week.
— Well, this is the third friend of ours that has vanished this year! I wonder what's going on?
— I don't know. Maybe our friends just have a new owner. Let's hope for the best. At least it's good to know that we will always be "man's best friend."

They must be lost dogs and so hungry and tired. If I attract them with this bone, they'll think I'm their new owner, a kind and generous man.

Topic Preview:

Do you think it is morally acceptable to eat any kind of animal? What agency in your country's government is responsible for food safety? Do they inspect every kind of food that is produced (i.e., all types of meat, fish, fruits, and vegetables)? What is the most unusual thing that you have ever eaten? Are there any types of food that you would never eat?

Dialogue:

Susan: Edward, I heard that you used to teach English in Korea.

Edward: Yeah, that's right. I taught at a university in Seoul for two years.

Susan: That sounds interesting. What was it like?

Edward: Well, the food was spicy, the traffic was heavy, and the students were nice.

Susan: That sounds like a good experience.

Edward: Yeah, it was. I miss Korea, and sometimes I think about going back.

Susan: By the way, did you ever eat any dog meat while you were there?

Edward: No, never!

Susan: Why not?

Edward: The first reason is simply that the production of dog meat is not inspected by any government agency, unlike beef and pork. That's the only reason I need.

Susan: I see. Well, I heard that eating dog meat is a dying custom in Korea anyway.

Edward: That's true. The Korean National Assembly recently passed a law that will shut down the dog meat trade. According to the new law, anyone who slaughters a dog for food will be punished by up to three years in prison or a very heavy fine.

Susan: Wow! It sounds as though they are really serious about ending this practice.

Edward: You are absolutely right about that.

Dog Meat

The objections to eating dog meat are threefold. First, the processing of dogs for food is not inspected by any Korean government officials. Between 1975 and 1978, dogs briefly had the legal status of livestock animals, but for the most part, dogs have not been approved as meat in Korea. Therefore, there is no government agency that inspects dog farms and dog meat production to ensure food safety.

A second objection lies in the manner in which dogs are slaughtered for food. According to international standards, all animals that are killed for food must first be rendered unconscious. In the case of cows and pigs, a stun gun is first used to immobilize the animal. Only after that is the animal's life taken. Korean dog meat producers do not use stun guns. The current method of dog slaughter is apparently the use of electrocution while the animal is still conscious (stopdogslaughter.com).

Finally, dogs have been genetically manipulated by human beings over a period of at least 15,000 years in order to transform them into companion animals. It has been proved that dogs and the gray wolf share 99.96% of their DNA. However, scientific research has shown that dogs are much more than domesticated wolves. Dogs have been genetically altered to desire human companionship.

Korean defenders of eating dog meat reject all of the above objections as invalid. They say that eating dog meat is a Korean tradition that should be preserved. However, it seems that the practice of eating dog meat is on the way out. In early 2024, the Korean parliament passed a bill banning the breeding and slaughter of dogs for food. Violators of the new law can be punished with up to three years in prison or a fine of up to 30 million Korean won ($23,000).

ISSUE 06 DOG MEAT

Vocabulary & Expressions:

livestock
* animals (such as cows, horses, and pigs) kept or raised, especially on a farm and for profit
  - Many people criticize modern methods of *livestock* farming as inhumane.

slaughter
* to kill and prepare animals for food
  - If we are going to eat animals for food, we should raise them and *slaughter* them in a humane manner.

render
* to cause to be or become
  - When my sister received the prize for top math student in her class, she was *rendered* speechless.

stun gun
* a weapon that uses an electric shock to disable an animal or person
  - A Taser is one type of *stun gun*.

immobilize
* to keep someone or something from moving
  - Before a major surgery, a doctor gives a patient a drug to *immobilize* them.

electrocution
* the killing of an animal or person using an electric shock
  - In 2020, a total of 17 people died in the US from *electrocution* by lightning.

manipulate
* to change or adapt something to suit one's purpose or advantage
  - Most dog breeds have been developed in the last 150 years, as dog breeders *manipulated* dogs' DNA to show certain characteristics.

transform
* to change completely
  - Through hard work and creativity, Koreans *transformed* their country into an economic powerhouse.

alter
* to change partly but not completely. Not to be confused with *altar*, which refers to a raised platform or table where people worship God.
  - People who are shy often *alter* their personality a little to succeed in the modern business world.

invalid
* being without a foundation in fact, logic, truth, or law
  - The judge rejected the lawyer's argument as *invalid*.

preserve
* to maintain or continue
  - Respect for elders is a custom that is still *preserved* in most Asian countries.

on the way out
* becoming no longer popular
  - Full-size cars are *on the way out*.

Open to Debate (1): 30 Korean Issues

● ● ● ● Open to Debate (1): *30 Korean Issues*

● Discussion Points:

1. Which of the arguments against eating dog meat do you think is the most persuasive?
2. Korean supporters of eating dog meat say that the practice is a Korean tradition that should continue. Do you think this view is strong and valid?
3. Do you think that the new law banning dog meat will succeed? Will dog meat consumers create a hidden market where they can secretly buy or eat dog meat?
4. Do you think dog meat has any special benefits that you cannot get from any other kind of meat?
5. Have you, or someone you know, ever eaten dog meat? What was the situation?

Read the following quotes about dogs.
Can you explain what they mean? Do you agree with the idea expressed?

6. A dog is the only thing on Earth that loves you more than he loves himself. Josh Billings
7. Dogs never bite me—just humans. Marilyn Monroe

● **Current Hot Topic: What to Do with Two Million Dogs**

The new law gives dog meat producers a three-year grace period to close down their business. However, two serious issues have emerged. First, dog meat producers are demanding a payment of $1,500 for each dog that they own, an amount the government claims is excessive. Second, dog farmers have asked what they are supposed to do with the two million dogs living on dog farms. The government has responded by saying that farmers who abandon or euthanize their dogs will face stiff penalties. Meanwhile, dog meat producers have threatened to release the remaining dogs in front of the presidential office.

● **For Further Discussion:**

1. Dog meat producers are angry that the new law has ended their livelihood. Should the Korean government compensate them? How much money should the farmers receive for each dog?
2. What should happen to the two million dogs that are now left on dog farms? It is unlikely that they can all be adopted, so is it acceptable to euthanize them?

Issue 06 ● Dog Meat   33

— You'd better stop drinking. Your health seems to be deteriorating.
— I know. That's why I make a vow to quit drinking every day.
— Why are you still drinking then?
— Because I always make the pledge to quit drinking when I'm drunk. Then I don't remember it next day.

He's right. I've never seen him swear when he's sober. He seems afraid that he can't keep his promise.

Topic Preview:

Do you drink alcohol? When did you take your first drink? Do you respect people who choose not to drink alcohol? Could you ever join a religion that prohibits alcohol? Would you ever live in a country that prohibits alcohol?

Dialogue:

Sarah: Hey, George. How do you like your job teaching English in Korea?

George: I like it very much. I teach at a university, and the students are very smart and polite.

Sarah: I see. Well, have you participated in the infamous Korean drinking culture?

George: No, not at all. I drink very little alcohol, but I have a lot of students who drink alcohol.

Sarah: Hmmm… you must have many stories to tell.

George: Yeah, I do. During my first semester teaching at the university, a student told me that he would be absent from class the following Friday because he was going on "M.T."

Sarah: What's M.T.?

George: That's exactly what I asked. He said it stands for "membership training," so I thought it must involve some type of instruction about college life.

Sarah: Oh? That's not what it means?

George: No. I found out that all they do during M.T. is drink alcohol and play games.

Sarah: Haha! That doesn't sound like any kind of training at all.

George: You are absolutely right. I started saying that M.T. really stands for "*maegju* training," which means "beer training."

Sarah: Very funny!

34 ■ Open to Debate (1): 30 Korean Issues

Drinking Culture

Drinking plays a small part in North American business situations. For example, if a company holds a Christmas party for employees, alcohol may be available. However, perhaps a third of the attendees will not drink any alcohol at all. They will be teetotalers for religious, health, or medical reasons. Any attempt to force them to drink alcohol would be considered highly offensive. Others will drink moderately, maybe having a glass of wine or a cocktail. In most situations like this, it is unlikely that any employee will get drunk. CEOs and managers would look askance at any employee who cannot control his intake of alcohol at a corporate event.

When international businesspeople come to Korea to do business, they find that the situation with respect to alcohol is totally different. The Korean working culture actually encourages and supports drinking. Many companies hold weekly work dinners called *hoesik*. These corporate get-togethers are viewed as a means of promoting bonding among team members. Thus, employees cannot shirk the responsibility of attending. During these dinners, bosses offer drinks to employees, and it is inconceivable for an employee to say no. If the boss drinks heavily, the employee is expected to follow suit.

While the drinking culture of Korean companies may have the noble goal of promoting team spirit, the practice often produces negative consequences. The Ministry of Gender Equality and Family conducted a study that concluded that *hoesik* was the occasion where most cases of sexual harassment occurred. A few years ago, a dean of Korea Polytechnic University was fired because of sexual harassment that occurred during and after an episode of *hoesik*. He sued the university in court, but he lost his case. Not surprisingly, the cases of sexual harassment decreased when *hoesik* was curtailed during the COVID-19 pandemic.

ISSUE 07 DRINKING CULTURE

Vocabulary & Expressions:

play a part   *to be involved in; to be a factor in
- Alcohol *plays a part* in many traffic accidents.

teetotaler   *describing a person who does not ever drink alcohol
- My grandfather was a *teetotaler*; he never drank alcohol.

moderately   *observing reasonable limits; avoiding extremes of behavior
- My mother always eats *moderately*, so she never gains weight.

look askance   *to view with mistrust or suspicion; to be doubtful about
- When my uncle said he made a million dollars in the stock market, my dad *looked askance* at him.

with respect to   *in relation to
- The two groups were similar *with respect to* age, sex, and diagnoses.

get-together   *an informal social gathering
- My family usually has a *get-together* at least once a month.

bonding   *the forming of a close relationship
- If a teacher is kind, her students will experience *bonding* with her.

shirk   *to avoid doing an obligation, especially because of laziness, fear, or dislike
- My father used to get angry at my brother when he *shirked* his chores.

inconceivable   *impossible to imagine or believe
- To live in a world without music is *inconceivable*.

follow suit   *to follow an example set by someone else
- When my dad stopped smoking, my uncle *followed suit*.

noble   *showing admirable or excellent qualities
- Many modern CEOs follow the *noble* goal of hiring more women.

curtail   *to reduce, diminish; to cut short
- My free time with friends was greatly *curtailed* during the COVID-19 pandemic.

●●●● *Open to Debate (1): 30 Korean Issues*

● *Discussion Points:*

1. Why is drinking such an important part of Korean business and society?
2. Have you ever participated in Korea's drinking culture? What was your experience like?
3. Korea has a complicated system of exchanging glasses when drinking. Do you think this custom should be stopped because of the danger of viruses, such as hepatitis?
4. Has anyone ever tried to force you to drink alcohol? How did you respond to the pressure?
5. Do you know anyone who does not drink alcohol at all? What are their reasons?

Read the following quotes about alcohol.
Can you explain what they mean? Do you agree with the idea expressed?

6. Drink because you are happy, but never because you are miserable.
   G. K. Chesterton
7. First you take a drink, then the drink takes a drink, then the drink takes you.
   F. Scott Fitzgerald

● **Current Hot Topic: Celebrities and DUI**

In 2022, actress Kim Sae-ron crashed into an electric transformer box while driving under the influence of alcohol (DUI). She fled the scene but was soon arrested. She issued an apology two days later, but her public image was severely damaged. Other celebrities whose reputation was harmed by DUI include Lizzy, a member of the girl group After School, and former AB6IX member Lim Young-min. On the other hand, veteran actor Lee Jung-jae, of *Squid Game* fame, enjoys immense popularity both domestically and globally, despite the fact that he has had two counts of DUI, in 1999 and 2002.

● **For Further Discussion:**

1. What punishment should be faced by celebrities who are arrested for DUI? Should they lose their jobs in entertainment, or should their cases be handled routinely like anyone else's?
2. Can you think of any other celebrities or politicians who were arrested for DUI? What happened to their careers?

— Are you taking health supplements?
— Yes, I take a multiple vitamin, protein powder, and omega-3 supplement. How about you?
— I take lots of supplements too.
— What do you take?
— I take milk, meat, fish, eggs, and lots of fruits and vegetables.
— They're not really supplements, are they?
— Yes, they are! They are NATURAL supplements.

Dog: As I age, my health is deteriorating, so I've been taking doggie vitamin pills and protein supplements, but I don't think my health is improving. I'm now considering taking human supplements. But I'm afraid of some side effects when I take them. Is there any difference between doggie and human supplements?

Topic Preview:

Many doctors say that if you simply eat good foods, you don't need to take vitamins and health supplements. Do you agree with this idea? Has a doctor or nurse ever told you that you should take a certain vitamin? Did you follow their advice? Do you know anyone who likes to take many vitamins and health supplements? What is their life like?

Dialogue:

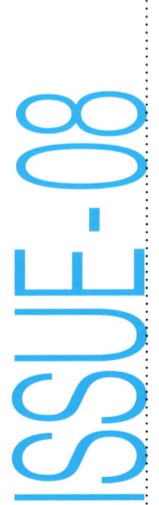

Sandra: Brian, do you take any health supplements?

Brian: No, I don't. My mother is a registered dietitian. She always told me that if you eat nutritious food, you don't need to take vitamins or supplements.

Sandra: I see. Well, I wonder why so many people think they have to take supplements.

Brian: I think it's because they are afraid that they're not eating enough good food.

Sandra: Yeah, you're probably right about that.

Brian: Also, there is a lot of misinformation being published about health supplements.

Sandra: Can you cite an example?

Brian: Sure. A few years ago, the government advised people not to use a product called "Slimming Plus Advanced," which was promoted as a weight loss supplement.

Sandra: You mean it didn't really help people to lose weight?

Brian: No, the pill was worse than that. It contained illegal ingredients that cause high blood pressure and cancer.

Sandra: Oh my! I guess I had better read what the experts say about any health supplement that I take.

Brian: Yes, of course. That's a very wise decision.

38 Open to Debate (1): 30 Korean Issues

Health Supplements

An American English teacher was working in Korea as an English teacher. One day a student gave him a small bottle of a brown liquid. The student explained, "You should drink it. It's good for your health." The teacher obliged and drank the contents of the little bottle. Later, the teacher visited a Korean pharmacy, and he saw an interesting sight: many Koreans bought health drinks, drank them on the spot, and then placed the empty bottle in the box for recycling. He realized then that Koreans take health drinks and health supplements very seriously.

The market for health supplements in Korea has increased dramatically over the past few decades. For example, one 40-something office worker takes pills to lower blood pressure and cholesterol every morning, along with vitamin C pills. Then he takes "milk thistle," which is promoted by health supplement advocates as a good dietary supplement for liver problems, diabetes, and even indigestion. The worker also takes three additional vitamin C pills at both lunch and dinner. He claims that he is in excellent health and will continue to take health supplements. According to one recent poll, about 85% of Koreans said that they have been taking health supplements. The Korean market for health supplements is expected to exceed 25 trillion won by 2030. It's very clear that taking health supplements has become an integral part of many Koreans' daily lives, just like eating and exercising.

The most important question with respect to health supplements is simple: is there scientific proof that they can actually improve your health? In reality, the scientific evidence for the benefits of vitamins and other supplements is mixed. Indeed, some supplements can be toxic at high doses. Some doctors say if you eat a healthy diet, you don't need supplements at all.

ISSUE 08　HEALTH SUPPLEMENTS

Vocabulary & Expressions:

oblige
* to do a favor for someone
  - When my friend asked me to take him to the airport, I was happy to **oblige**.

on the spot
* right away; immediately
  - The job applicant was so skilled that the manager hired her **on the spot**.

take seriously
* to treat someone or something as being very important and deserving special attention and respect
  - My grandparents go to church every Sunday; they **take** their religious faith very **seriously**.

-something
* a suffix used to indicate an approximate number
  - I don't know my teacher's exact age, but I think she's 50-**something**.

advocate
* a person who supports an idea, plan, cause, or product
  - Many students are **advocates** for less homework.

diabetes
* a disease in which a person has high blood sugar
  - My uncle has **diabetes**, so he has to take insulin every day.

indigestion
* an upset stomach caused by slow or painful digestion of food
  - I can't eat too much spicy food because it causes **indigestion** for me.

integral
* very important and necessary; needed to make something complete
  - My family members are dedicated Buddhists; going to the temple is an **integral** part of our lives.

mixed
* including a combination of positive and negative aspects
  - I had **mixed** feelings about moving to Australia to study English.

toxic
* harmful and poisonous
  - Tylenol is a helpful pain reliever, but it can be **toxic** if you take too much.

dose
* a measured amount of medicine to be used at one time
  - My father takes medicine to lower his cholesterol; the **dose** is one 40-milligram pill per day.

●●●● *Open to Debate (1): 30 Korean Issues*

● *Discussion Points:*

1. Do you take any type of vitamins or health supplements? Why do you take them?
2. Are health drinks popular in your country? Which ones do you like?
3. How can you be sure that you are not taking too much of a vitamin or other supplement?
4. Do you know anyone who refuses to take any kind of health supplement? What reasons do they give for their refusal?

Read the following quotes about vitamins and health supplements.
Can you explain what they mean? Do you agree with the idea expressed?

5. A healthful, well-balanced diet that includes whole grains will provide sufficient vitamins and minerals for the vast majority of people.
   Dr. JoAnn E. Manson
6. I don't take supplements—I get nutrition from food. Maye Musk
7. I take a vitamin every day; it's called a steak. Robert Duvall

● *Current Hot Topic:* **Vegetarianism in Korea**

It seems that few Koreans are willing to become vegetarians to achieve good health. A recent survey asked more than 5,500 Koreans about their meat consumption. The results of the survey indicated that only 418 respondents (7.6%) followed some type of meat-restrictive diet. Some avoided red meat but still ate chicken; others, called pescetarians, avoided chicken and red meat but ate fish. Only 13 respondents, which represented 0.2% of the group, avoided eating all types of meat. Only two respondents claimed to be vegans, a term that refers to people who avoid all types of meat, dairy products, and eggs.

● *For Further Discussion:*

1. Do you know any vegetarians or vegans? What is their life like?
2. Could you ever become a vegetarian? What about for just one day per week?

People fear death even more than pain. But I'm not afraid of death because death is a great relief. After death, I won't have to BOTHER to eat, sleep, study, work, exercise, worry, see doctors, or flatter anybody. The list of the advantages of death goes on and on, and finally the biggest advantage is that it can be done as easily as lying down.

Topic Preview:

What happens in your country when a person is unconscious and cannot recover from an illness? If you were in a coma for a long time, would you want your body to be kept alive by machines? What does it mean to "die with dignity"? Do you know anyone who has Alzheimer's disease? What is their life like?

Dialogue:

Patricia: Hey, Kevin. Do you have an advance health care directive?

Kevin: You mean that document that tells how you want to be treated if you're sick and have no chance of recovery?

Patricia: Yeah, that's what I'm talking about.

Kevin: No, I haven't signed one of those documents yet. I'm still young, so I don't think I need one.

Patricia: Well, what if you are seriously injured in a car accident?

Kevin: Hmmm... in that case, I might need one. By the way, do you have an advance directive?

Patricia: Yes, I do. My dad's a lawyer. He wrote one for everybody in my family.

Kevin: I see. Well, maybe I should get one. How much do they cost?

Patricia: They cost about $250, I think, but maybe my dad would give you a discount since you're my friend.

Kevin: Okay. I'll think about it. Thanks for the information.

High Cost of Dying

Dying in South Korea can take an emotional toll on families. A man named Mr. Chun was diagnosed with Alzheimer's disease and dementia. He now lives in a nursing home, but there is no hope for his recovery. Of course, his family comes to visit him, but they leave the home in a state of depression. He is not conscious most of the time, and when he is, he cannot even recognize his family or talk. About 80% of Koreans die in hospitals or nursing homes. In many cases, unconscious patients are kept alive by medical machines and go through months of pain before dying.

Korea became a superaged society in the late 2010s, which means that more than 20% of its population is over age 65. Experts say that the number of annual deaths in Korea is expected to reach 350,000 in 2025 and 500,000 in 2040. The life expectancy in Korea is now over 83 years of age, but the healthy life expectancy remains at only about 66 years, which means that many of the elderly can expect to live their last 17 years with deteriorating physical health.

One sensible way that people can prepare for death is by signing an "advance health care directive," AKA "a living will." In this legal document, a person specifies what actions they want taken in case they become incapacitated and unable to make their own medical decisions. Fortunately, Korea enacted such a "death with dignity" law in 2018, and more than a million people have signed this type of document. However, it is still illegal in Korea for any terminally ill person to take their own life, in spite of the fact that a survey showed that more than 75% of Koreans believe that euthanasia and physician-assisted suicide should be legal.

ISSUE 09 HIGH COST OF DYING

Vocabulary & Expressions:

take a toll
* to cause harm or damage to someone or something; also written as *take its toll*
  - If you work too hard for a long time, the stress will **take a toll** on your body.

diagnose
* to recognize a disease by its signs and symptoms
  - If you have a runny nose and a cough, your doctor may **diagnose** you with a cold.

dementia
* a condition where a person experiences progressive loss of memory, thinking, and normal behavior
  - Alzheimer's disease is one common cause of **dementia**.

deteriorate
* to make or become worse or less valuable
  - After my boyfriend lied to me, our relationship **deteriorated** quickly.

sensible
* showing wise judgment; reasonable
  - My mother is very **sensible** about money; she always spends money wisely.

AKA
* also known as
  - BTS, **AKA** "the Bangtan Boys," is one of the most popular boy bands in pop music history.

will
* a legal document in which a person states to whom his or her property should be given after death; short for *last will and testament*
  - If you die without a **will**, a court will decide what happens to your property and money.

incapacitated
* unable to act or respond
  - After a bad car accident, my cousin was unconscious and **incapacitated** for a week.

dignity
* the right of a person to be valued, respected, and treated properly
  - According to the United Nations, all human beings are born free and are equal in **dignity** and rights.

terminally ill
* describing a person with an incurable sickness that will lead to death
  - My grandfather had cancer and was **terminally** ill during the last six months of his life.

euthanasia
* the act of killing someone painlessly, especially to relieve suffering from an incurable illness; AKA *mercy killing*
  - In 2001, the Netherlands passed a law legalizing **euthanasia**, including physician-assisted suicide.

●●●● Open to Debate (1): *30 Korean Issues*

● **Discussion Points:**

1. Do you know anyone who has signed an advance health care directive? Would you like to sign one in the future?
2. Have you had any elderly relatives who died? How did they die? Do you think they "died with dignity"?
3. Do you think that Korea should allow euthanasia and physician-assisted suicide?
4. If you could choose your own manner of death, what type of death would you choose?

Read the following quotes about euthanasia.
Can you explain what they mean? Do you agree with the idea expressed?

5. Euthanasia is a grave violation of the law of God, since it is the deliberate and morally unacceptable killing of a human person. Pope John Paul II
6. One should die proudly when it is no longer possible to live proudly. Friedrich Nietzsche
7. The right to die can so easily become the duty to die. Peter Saunders

● **Current Hot Topic: The High Cost of Funerals**

A man named Mr. Gong faced an expensive situation when his father-in-law died, and the body was placed in the mortuary at a hospital. Following Korean custom, Mr. Gong prepared to buy a funeral shroud, called a *su-ui* in Korean. Hospital officials pressured him to buy the shroud from the hospital service, at a cost of $5,000. However, Mr. Gong argued with the officials about the price, and he finally bought the funeral shroud from another source, for about $1,000. According to Korean law, funeral items can be purchased from any source, but some hospitals do not follow this law.

● **For Further Discussion:**

1. Do you know anyone who had an experience like that of Mr. Gong? How can hospitals force families to buy all funeral items from the hospital, when this practice is clearly illegal?
2. What is the total cost of a funeral with a traditional burial in your country? How much does cremation cost? Why not just donate your body to medical science and save the funeral costs altogether?

— If you buy my house, I guarantee that the price will skyrocket, and you'll be able to resell it with a huge profit.
— But I'm afraid it will burst all of a sudden in my hands. It seems like a game of Russian roulette.
— Don't worry. I'm sure it won't burst until somebody buys it.

The bubble is getting bigger and bigger, so there's a great possibility that it will burst when it's finally mine. But I'm sure I'll be remembered at least as a great Russian roulette player.

Topic Preview:

Do you think that buying a house or apartment is a good investment? How can you know the best time to buy a house? Do you know anyone who bought a house but then couldn't pay for it? What happened? Do you hope to buy a house in the future? How much do you expect to pay?

Dialogue:

Nancy: Hey, Joshua. I heard you got married. Congratulations!

Joshua: Thank you, Nancy! We got married last month. So far, married life is going very well.

Nancy: That's great! Where are you two living?

Joshua: We live on the east side of the city.

Nancy: Are you buying a home?

Joshua: No, not at all. We can't afford to buy a house right now. We are just renting a two-bedroom apartment.

Nancy: I see. Well, my husband and I are doing the same thing. It's just too expensive to buy a house these days.

Joshua: You are so right. Also, you never know if it's the right time to buy a house.

Nancy: That's really true. You could end up in a housing bubble that bursts, and then your house is worth less than you paid for it.

Joshua: You are absolutely right! That's why we're just renting for right now. Maybe we'll buy a house in a few years.

Nancy: Good strategy!

Housing Bubble

Most people think of real estate as a wise investment. The stock market is unpredictable, and the price of gold fluctuates widely. However, if you buy property, such as a house or office building, it is bound to go up in price after some time. These ideas seem reasonable until you realize one simple fact: if there is a housing bubble, real estate prices will eventually collapse, and investors will lose their money. The word "bubble" is often used to describe a state of booming economic activity in the stock market, real estate, or technology. In real life, all bubbles eventually burst, and the same thing happens with investments.

One Korean couple found out firsthand exactly what it's like to participate in a housing bubble. They moved from Korea to the United States with their two children in 2006, and they immediately started a business. Remembering that real estate is usually a great investment, they bought a large and expensive house. Unbeknownst to them, the world was about to enter the global financial crisis of 2007–2008. Only a year after they bought their house, it plummeted in value, and at the same time, their business began to decline. They had no choice but to declare bankruptcy and move out of their nice house into an apartment. They survived but sadly their American dream turned into a financial nightmare.

In mid-2021, the Bank of Korea (BOK) warned that the country may be in the midst of a housing bubble. Apartment prices in Seoul surged more than 90% during the presidency of Moon Jae-in, and rising housing prices showed no signs of stabilizing. To make matters worse, household debt increased to more than $1.5 trillion. The BOK warned that the housing bubble could eventually collapse, triggering a financial crisis.

ISSUE 10 HOUSING BUBBLE

Vocabulary & Expressions:

real estate   *property consisting of buildings and land
- Many people buy houses because they think *real estate* is a good investment.

unpredictable   *impossible to predict; not able to be known in advance
- The stock market is *unpredictable*; the stocks you buy can go up or down.

fluctuate   *to go up and down
- The price of oil has *fluctuated* widely this year.

bound   *sure, certain, destined
- If the hurricane hits Miami, it is *bound* to cause a lot of damage.

collapse   *to suddenly lose value, force, or significance
- The country's economy *collapsed* because of its high debts and inflation.

booming   *growing or expanding very quickly
- A new pizza restaurant in our neighborhood has been doing a *booming* business since it opened.

burst   *to break open, apart, or into pieces
- When children play with balloons, the balloons usually *burst* after a few minutes.

firsthand   *obtained from direct personal experience
- When you lose your job, you learn *firsthand* what it means to have no income.

unbeknownst   *happening without someone's knowledge; unknown
- *Unbeknownst* to my mother, we planned a surprise party for her 60th birthday.

plummet   *to drop sharply and suddenly
- When the technology bubble burst in the early 2000s, prices of technology stocks *plummeted*.

bankruptcy   *the situation of not having enough money to pay debts
- After my uncle lost his job, he could not pay his debts and had to declare *bankruptcy*.

stabilize   *to become firm, steadfast, and unlikely to change suddenly
- A housing bubble is always a danger until home prices *stabilize*.

Open to Debate (1): 30 Korean Issues

Discussion Points:

1. Who is mostly to blame for a housing bubble: the banks, the government, or the people?
2. One way to protect yourself against a housing bubble is simply to rent a house instead of buying. Do you think that's a good idea?
3. Experts seem unable to predict exactly when a housing bubble will occur. Why do you think this is true?
4. What actions can the government take to avoid a housing bubble or make it less harmful?
5. Does your family own a house or any other property? Do you think it has been a good investment?
6. Where is the best place to buy a home in your city? How much would a nice home or apartment cost?
7. If you suddenly received $10,000, would you invest it in real estate, the stock market, gold, or something else?

Current Hot Topic: The Cause and Effect of Consumer Debt

In 2008, the ratio of household debt to income in Korea was about 138%. By 2020, it was over 200%. Why have Koreans accumulated such a high amount of household debt? According to some experts, Koreans are excessive consumers. They work many hours in order to reach a certain level of lifestyle. When their salary is not enough, they borrow money. Unfortunately, several years of the COVID-19 pandemic have only worsened the situation. As a result of the dire economic situation, many young people have had to give up the idea of starting a family or even getting married.

For Further Discussion:

1. Why do you think many Koreans have such a high amount of household debt? What is the best way to avoid this situation from happening?
2. Do you know any young people who have given up the idea of starting a family or getting married? What is their life like?

I was lucky I could get this job as a garbageman—all because local people truly hate 3-D jobs. I'm now working happily with a relatively higher wage, and I can commute to work in my BMW sedan.

I'm now wrestling with my computer in the office all day long, while just earning minimum wage. But my personal vanity won't allow me to work on a 3-D job. I'm happily commuting with my bicycle, and on the positive side, it makes me stronger.

I know his remarks are nothing but sour grapes.

🟢 Topic Preview:

How often do you see an international worker in your country? What kinds of jobs do they do? Can Korea solve its shortage of workers simply by bringing in more foreign workers? Some Koreans say that the only reason international workers come to Korea is because "they failed in their home countries." Do you think this claim is true?

🟡 Dialogue:

Michelle: Kenneth, how do you like teaching English in Korea? You've been working there for two years, right?

Kenneth: Yeah, that's right. I'm just here in the US on summer vacation now, and yes, I enjoy teaching English there very much.

Michelle: So do you plan to make it your career?

Kenneth: That's possible, but I'm still in my twenties, so I haven't made such a long-term commitment.

Michelle: I see. Have you thought about becoming a Korean citizen?

Kenneth: I have thought about it, but not seriously. The requirements are a little strict. I would have to live there for five years and also score well on the Korean language exam.

Michelle: Korean seems like a difficult language for English speakers to learn.

Kenneth: Yeah, I think it is. Also, if I became a Korean citizen, I would have to give up my American citizenship.

Michelle: Wow! I didn't know that. They won't allow you to have dual citizenship?

Kenneth: No, not at all. I wouldn't become a Korean citizen unless I planned to live there for the rest of my life.

Michelle: I see. Well, you have plenty of time to make that decision.

International Workers

The COVID-19 pandemic took its toll on people's health in Korea, but it also led to a decrease in the number of international workers in the country. According to Statistics Korea, in 2021, a total of 221,000 foreigners arrived in Korea to work or study and 263,000 left, adding up to a net loss of 43,000. The net outflow of foreigners in their 30s totaled 28,000 and 12,000 for those in their 40s. It is not surprising that a recent survey of 10,000 small and midsize enterprises (SMEs) revealed that 57% said they were short of workers. This shortage has been a matter of growing concern for the Korean government since the pandemic started.

Many jobs remain unfulfilled at SMEs because Korean young people turn up their noses at such positions. They would rather remain unemployed than to take jobs that they consider beneath their dignity. They are unwilling to work on 3-D jobs, as their grandparents did in the 1950s and 1960s. About 70% of Koreans between the ages of 25 and 34 have a college degree, the highest level among all the OECD member countries. These well-educated college graduates prefer to work only for a large company, a public institution, or a government department.

Because of the shortage of workers, the Korean government is mulling over the possibility of creating a special visa category that would attract foreign workers. The new visa would have more relaxed requirements than current visas. In addition, the Korean government is now allowing special nonscheduled flights to bring in migrant workers from various countries. Korea has no choice but to bring in more foreign workers. By 2070, Korea's population will shrink from its current level of 50+ million to 38 million, and the workforce will drop from 37 million to just 17 million.

ISSUE 11 INTERNATIONAL WORKERS

Vocabulary & Expressions:

net loss
*an amount or number that is lost
- Last year at my college, 500 students graduated and only 400 new students were admitted, so the college had a *net loss* of 100 students.

enterprise
*a business organization or activity
- Mr. Wilson started seven *enterprises*, several of which earned a lot of money.

short of
*having less than what you need of something
- I've spent all my money, so I'm a little *short of* cash right now.

matter
*an issue that must be dealt with or considered
- The students complained about too much homework, so the teacher had to deal with the *matter*.

turn up one's nose
*to regard something or someone with a feeling of strong dislike
- My little sister *turned up her nose* at the broccoli, refusing to eat it.

beneath one's dignity
*considering yourself too important to do something that is unpleasant or unimportant
- My father worked hard on his job, so he thought that cleaning the bathroom at home was *beneath his dignity*.

3-D job
*a job that is "dirty, dangerous, and difficult" (or "dirty, dangerous, and demanding" or "dirty, dangerous, and demeaning")
- The term *3-D job* originated from a Japanese expression that was used to describe difficult jobs that were performed by foreign workers.

OECD
*Organisation for Economic Co-operation and Development
- The *OECD* has almost 40 members, all of which are highly developed democratic countries.

mull over
*to think about something slowly and carefully
- I asked my girlfriend to marry me, but she wants some time to *mull over* the decision.

attract
*to cause others to be interested in something
- The British Museum *attracts* over six million visitors every year.

relaxed
*easy; not strict; informal
- At my office, we have a *relaxed* atmosphere; it's okay to wear casual clothes.

migrant
*a person who moves regularly in order to find work in other countries
- The United States accepts many *migrant* workers who pick fruit and work on farms.

Open to Debate (1): 30 Korean Issues

Discussion Points:

1. Do you know any college graduates who refuse to take a 3-D job? What are their reasons?
2. Why aren't college graduates willing to take a job in an SME? What's so bad about working in that type of business?
3. Do you think the Korean government is doing enough to attract international workers to Korea? What else could they do?
4. Do you think that international workers in Korea are well treated? Have you heard of any examples where they were mistreated?
5. Have you read any stories about migrants who were working illegally without a visa in Korea? What happened to them?

Read the following quotes about migrant workers.
Can you explain what they mean? Do you agree with the idea expressed?

6. Migration is an expression of the human aspiration for dignity, safety, and a better future. It is part of the social fabric, part of our very make-up as a human family. Ban Ki-moon
7. The greatest nations are defined by how they treat their weakest inhabitants. Jorge Ramos

Current Hot Topic: Citizenship for International Workers

Foreign residents in Korea who are over age 20 can become naturalized Korean citizens after living in the country for five years and achieving at least a level 4 score on the government's Korean language proficiency exam. Foreigners who become Korean citizens must give up their previous citizenship within one year. However, individuals who have made exceptional contributions to Korea may be exempted from this requirement by the Ministry of Justice. Naturalization was very rare until 2000. Since then, more than 200,000 foreign residents have become Korean citizens. This number will certainly increase as more foreign workers come to Korea.

For Further Discussion:

1. Would you like to see more international workers become Korean citizens? Why doesn't the Korean government allow new citizens to keep their previous country's citizenship?
2. Have you ever thought about moving to live and work in another country? Which country? Would you try to become a citizen of that country?

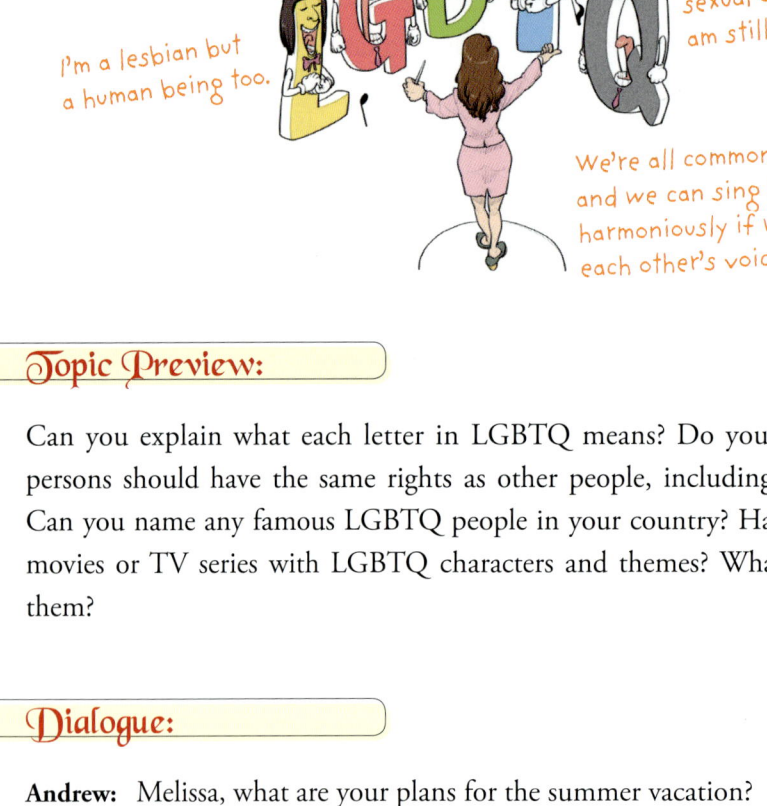

⬤ Topic Preview:

Can you explain what each letter in LGBTQ means? Do you think that LGBTQ persons should have the same rights as other people, including the right to marry? Can you name any famous LGBTQ people in your country? Have you ever seen any movies or TV series with LGBTQ characters and themes? What is your opinion of them?

⬤ Dialogue:

Andrew: Melissa, what are your plans for the summer vacation?

Melissa: I'll be going to my brother's wedding in New Zealand.

Andrew: Oh, wow! That's nice. Where is his wife-to-be from?

Melissa: You mean husband-to-be. My brother is gay.

Andrew: Oh, sorry. I didn't know. Well, where is his husband-to-be from?

Melissa: He's from South Korea. They met at the University of Auckland.

Andrew: I see. Well, don't they want to get married in Korea?

Melissa: Actually, that's impossible. Korea does not allow same-sex marriage.

Andrew: And New Zealand does?

Melissa: Yes, that's right. New Zealand approved same-sex marriage in 2013.

Andrew: I see. Well, congratulations to your brother and his new husband, and enjoy your visit to New Zealand.

Melissa: Thanks! I'll be sure to bring you back a New Zealand souvenir.

Andrew: That sounds great, thanks!

LGBTQ

Lee Kyung-eun, born in 1975, knew from early childhood that he had the mindset of a female. Therefore, he underwent sex reassignment surgery in the 1990s and became Harisu, now widely known as South Korea's first transgender entertainer. In 2002, Harisu became the second person in Korea to legally change their gender. Harisu gained public attention in 2001, when she appeared in a TV commercial for DoDo cosmetics. Soon she branched out into other fields, including music and acting. In 2007, Harisu married Mickey Jung, a rapper whom she met online. The couple divorced in 2017.

Many people thought that the widespread acceptance of Harisu by Korean society heralded a new era in Korea, where the rights of LGBTQ individuals would be protected. In fact, the legal status of homosexuality as "harmful and obscene" was officially abolished in 2003. In 2014, Korea voted in favor of a United Nations resolution that opposed violence and discrimination against "LGBT individuals." In spite of these hopeful signs, the LGBTQ community in Korea still faces discrimination. Same-sex couples cannot marry in Korea or even have a civil union. In addition, the government provides no antidiscrimination protections, nor does it prohibit hate crimes based on sexual orientation.

In May 2019, a Korean woman named Kim Gyu-Jin married her wife in New York City. Later, they also had a marriage ceremony in Korea. However, when they filed a marriage registration form with the Jongno-gu Office, their petition was denied. Kim talked about her experience on KakaoTalk, Korea's leading messaging app. The article received about 10,000 comments, 80% of which were negative. Some commenters even told the couple to "get out of Korea." On the other hand, in a recent survey, the percentage of Koreans who oppose homosexuality fell below 50% for the first time.

ISSUE 12 LGBTQ

Vocabulary & Expressions:

mindset — *a mental attitude or mood; an outlook or way of looking at life
- My sister has always had a *mindset* of helping people, so she became a nurse.

sex reassignment surgery — *a surgical procedure by which a transgender person's physical appearance is changed to resemble that of their gender identity; AKA *gender reassignment surgery* or *gender confirmation surgery*
- Alicia Liu was born as a male in Taiwan, but after undergoing *sex reassignment surgery* at age 18, she became a model and TV personality.

branch out — *to begin to do different kinds of activities or work
- Samsung started as a trading company in 1938, but they soon *branched out* into many other areas of business.

herald — *to foretell; to indicate the coming of something new
- Yuri Gagarin of Russia became the first person to fly into outer space in 1961; his flight *heralded* a new age of space exploration.

LGBTQ — *lesbian, gay, bisexual, transgender, questioning (or queer)
- Many variations of *LGBTQ* exist, including *LGBTQ+*, where the "+" represents those whose identity is not covered in *LGBTQ*.

homosexuality — *sexual or romantic attraction to others of the same sex; the state of being gay
- Nowadays, most gay people are offended by the terms *homosexuality* and *homosexual*; it's more polite to refer to them as *gay*.

obscene — *very shocking and offensive according to people's sense of what is moral, right, and decent
- In some places, kissing in public is considered *obscene* behavior.

resolution — *a formal statement of the opinion, will, or intent of an official group
- On September 17, 1991, the United Nations admitted both North Korea and South Korea into UN membership under *Resolution* 46/1.

discrimination — *the process of unfairly treating a person or group differently from other people
- The law clearly prohibits *discrimination* against the disabled.

civil union — *a legal status that ensures to same-sex couples some of the rights and responsibilities of married couples
- Hungary recognizes same-sex *civil unions* but not same-sex marriages.

sexual orientation — *a person's sexual identity as straight, gay, bisexual, and so forth
- It's much better to use the term *sexual orientation* than the term *sexual preference*.

petition — *a formal written request made to a governmental authority
- If you want to take legal action, you will have present a *petition* to a court.

● ● ● ● *Open to Debate (1): 30 Korean Issues*

Discussion Points:

1. Why has South Korea been so slow to accept LGBTQ people and to pass laws to protect their human rights?
2. Do you think that Korea will ever allow same-sex marriage? When do you think that will happen?
3. How would you feel if one of your friends suddenly announced that he or she is LGBTQ? Do you have any LGBTQ friends now?
4. Do you think that LGBTQ persons can serve in any job in your country, including the military?

Read the following quotes about the LGBTQ community.
Can you explain what they mean? Do you agree with the idea expressed?

5. Nature made a mistake, which I have corrected. Christine Jorgensen, one of the first Americans to have sex reassignment surgery
6. When all Americans are treated as equal, no matter who they are or whom they love, we are all more free. Barack Obama
7. So let me be clear: I'm proud to be gay, and I consider being gay among the greatest gifts God has given me. Tim Cook, CEO of Apple

● **Current Hot Topic:** **Bringing "Boys' Love" into the Light**

In the past, Korean television series that featured LGBTQ themes have been dealt with harshly. In 2015, the JTBC series *Schoolgirl Detectives* received disciplinary action from the government because the series featured a same-sex kiss. In 2016, the lesbian-themed online series *Lily Fever* also received a strict response from the government. However, in early 2022, a new series entitled *Semantic Error* brought the genre of "boys' love" (BL) into prominence. The series features two young men who engage in a campus romance. So far, the government has not intervened. Perhaps this series will serve to ease some social prejudices.

● **For Further Discussion:**

1. Have you seen the series *Semantic Error*? If not, would you like to see it?
2. Do you think the government should allow TV series to feature LGBTQ themes without any interference? Or should the government censor such shows?

We're the last couple living in the world due to the low birth rate. We don't have any kids anymore.

Humans have been our boss for a long time, but now the human species is on the brink of extinction because of their low birth rate. Now it's our turn. Now is the time for us to rule the earth thanks to our active reproduction.

When it comes to reproduction, we're the best. We'll fill the earth with our babies in a couple of years. But I don't think we'll be able to be the king of the earth because of the cats.

Good! We don't have to worry about our food thanks to your high reproduction rate.

Topic Preview:

Have you read about the problem of low birth rates around the world? Do you think it's possible that some countries could simply disappear in the future? Which countries have the lowest birth rates? Which countries have the highest birth rates?

Dialogue:

Margaret: Steven, I heard that your wife is pregnant again.

Steven: Yes, that's right, Margaret. This will be our fourth child.

Margaret: Well, congratulations! That's wonderful.

Steven: Thanks very much. We're hoping for a boy this time. We already have three girls.

Margaret: Well, good luck with that. Nowadays, it's just unusual for a couple to have four children.

Steven: Well, I'm Canadian, and our nation's birth rate is only 1.4. We need a birth rate of 2.1 just to maintain the population.

Margaret: Wow! I had no idea that the birth rate in Canada was so low.

Steven: Well, my wife and I are just trying to do our part to increase the birth rate.

Margaret: Well, maybe you should go further and have twelve children, as a couple did in that 2003 film *Cheaper by the Dozen*.

Steven: Let's not go that far!

Margaret: I was kidding!

Low Birth Rate

In 2014, a Korean-American journalist named Euny Hong authored a captivating book entitled *The Birth of Korean Cool: How One Nation Is Conquering the World through Pop Culture*. Hong recounts how South Korea transformed itself from an impoverished country into a global leader in business, technology, education, and pop culture. According to the book's back cover, "*The Birth of Korean Cool* reveals how a really uncool country became cool, and how a nation that once banned miniskirts, long hair on men, and rock 'n' roll could come to mass-produce boy bands, soap operas, and the world's most important smartphone." Hong certainly proves her case, but sadly, experts say that there will come a time when Koreans no longer exist as a people.

In the same year that Hong penned her fascinating book, the Korean National Assembly commissioned a study of Korean population trends. The study concluded that South Koreans could "face natural extinction by 2750 if the birth rate were maintained at 1.19 children per woman." According to the research, South Korea's current population of slightly over 50 million could fall to 20 million by the year 2100. The city of Busan will vanish by 2413, and the capital, Seoul, will disappear by 2505.

These dire predictions may seem alarmist. However, current statistics prove that they are accurate. Simply to maintain a population, a country needs a birth rate of 2.1 babies per woman. The birth rate in Korea was only 0.92 in 2019, and in 2020, it fell to 0.84. The nation's capital, Seoul, had the lowest birth rate of only 0.64. Furthermore, in 2020, Korea recorded more deaths than births for the first time ever. From 1982 to 2016, a total of 3,725 schools in Korea closed due to a lack of students. The nation's workforce is likewise shrinking.

ISSUE 13 LOW BIRTH RATE

Vocabulary & Expressions:

captivating *attracting and holding a person's attention and interest because of excellence or beauty
- *The Godfather*, a **captivating** film from 1972, may be the best American movie of all time.

recount *to tell all about; to narrate
- My uncle often **recounted** his adventures of serving in the army.

impoverished *poor and needy
- My church helps **impoverished** people by giving away free meals and clothing.

uncool *not fashionable, sophisticated, or attractive; lacking in sophistication or self-confidence
- In high school, my cousin always looked **uncool** because he wore old clothes.

cool *fashionable, stylish, or attractive in a way that many people approve of
- When my cousin got his first girlfriend, he started to look really **cool** because she helped him choose nice, stylish clothes.

mass-produce *to create in large quantities, especially by machinery or a standard method
- The Ford Motor Company was one of the first companies to **mass-produce** cars.

soap opera *a television series showing the interconnected lives of many characters, often in a melodramatic or emotional manner
- The term **soap opera** was created because advertisers sold household products like soap to the many housewives who watched the TV programs.

prove one's case *to provide convincing evidence and arguments that a claim is true
- Scientists have clearly **proved their case** that the new virus is very dangerous.

extinction *the situation when something no longer exists
- Scientists say that the **extinction** of the dinosaurs occurred about 65 million years ago.

vanish *to pass from sight or existence; to disappear
- The magician caused a rabbit to **vanish** during the magic show.

dire *very urgent or serious
- Global warming is a **dire** problem faced by every country.

alarmist *a person who exaggerates dangers, causing others to feel a sense of danger or worry
- My uncle is such an **alarmist**; he says inflation will destroy our lives.

Open to Debate (1): 30 Korean Issues

Discussion Points:

1. Why does the birth rate in Korea continue to decrease?
2. What is the Korean government doing to increase the birth rate? How could they do better?
3. Do you think Korea should solve the problem of its low birth rate by welcoming more immigrants to the country? What are the pros and cons of this approach?
4. Should people feel sad about Korea's population decline, or should we simply accept it as nature's way or destiny?
5. How many brothers and sisters do you have? Do you wish you had more?
6. How many children would you like to have? Would you have more children if the government gave you money to help pay for them? How much money would you want per child?
7. How many children are in the largest family that you know? What is the largest family that you have heard about in your country?

Current Hot Topic: DINKs

Having children and raising them is very expensive. If you consider the total cost of raising a child from birth to age 18, the amount can easily top $250,000. If you support your child through college, the cost climbs even higher. Because of the huge expense of raising children, many young couples are choosing to have no kids at all. Such couples are called "DINKs," meaning "double income, no children." These couples have two incomes, and because they don't face the expense of raising children, they can have a more comfortable lifestyle. DINKs obviously contribute to Korea's low birth rate.

For Further Discussion:

1. What is your opinion of DINKs? Should we view them as selfish people or simply allow them to live as they want without any criticism?
2. DINK couples gain the benefit of having more money. What disadvantages does their lifestyle create?

We demand that South Korea break up with the United States and befriend us. Then we won't have to show hostility toward South Korea.

We're determined to develop nuclear weapons to defend our regime and to continue to launch missiles toward South Korea until they give us food and money.

We will increase our military power continuously, so someday soon we'll be able to wage a war against China and the United States. We want our country to become the number one power on Earth.

It's so sad that our country is geographically surrounded by belligerent nations, and we still don't have atomic bombs. Is having nuclear weapons the key to preserving our national sovereignty?

No, you have a very dangerous idea! Didn't we promise that Korea would always be under the umbrella of our nuclear power? We're always ready to help you if you engage in a war with any nations around you. You have nothing to worry about concerning your neighboring countries.

Topic Preview:

Which of South Korea's neighboring countries is your favorite? Why do you like them more than the others? Do you think South Korea and North Korea will ever be reunited? Many North Koreans have defected to South Korea, but some of them found life difficult in the South. Why do you think this is true?

Dialogue:

Paul: Lisa, I heard that you studied in South Korea.

Lisa: Yeah, that's right. I studied at Yonsei University in Seoul for a year. It was a special program for foreigners.

Paul: Wow! That sounds really cool. What did you learn?

Lisa: Well, I learned a lot about Korean culture and history, and I also learned to speak a little Korean.

Paul: Nice! Weren't you afraid of North Korea? They're always shooting off missiles and making threats.

Lisa: No, not at all. The South Korean military is very strong, and they also have the American military to back them up.

Paul: Yeah, that's true.

Lisa: I don't think North Korea would ever attack South Korea because they know they would lose, probably within a month.

Paul: I see. Well, it's interesting to hear your perspective.

Lisa: Yeah, I felt a lot safer in Seoul than I ever did in Chicago. The US has about 45,000 gun homicides per year. Korea has about 10.

Paul: I guess you're right. Korea sounds much safer.

North Korea, China, and Japan

South Korea has three powerful neighbors, and it has to try to get along with each one. Just across the DMZ is the belligerent neighbor, North Korea. After the Korean War ended in 1953, the relationship between the two countries continued to be very hostile. When Kim Dae-jung became president of South Korea in 1998, he tried to improve relations with North Korea through his "Sunshine Policy," and he won the Nobel Peace Prize for his efforts, though the positive effects turned out to be short lived. When Yoon Suk-yeol became president of South Korea in 2022, he promised to work favorably with North Korea if they would choose denuclearization.

China is South Korea's most important trading partner. China buys more than 25% of South Korea's exports, so the two countries have endeavored to promote a high-level relationship. Unfortunately, their relations suffered in 2016 when South Korea and the United States agreed to deploy a defense system called THAAD in response to missile threats from North Korea. China feared that the new system might be used by the US to contain China. In response, China decreased imports from South Korea. While trade between the two countries has rebounded, South Korea is trying to increase exports to other countries.

Japan and South Korea are competitive neighbors with a long history of disputes. Koreans have not forgotten that Japan ruled over Korea between 1910 and 1945 and that Japan turned large numbers of Korean women into sex slaves during World War II. In spite of these painful episodes and against much Korean opposition, President Park Chung-hee established diplomatic relations with Japan in 1965. The two countries successfully cohosted the 2002 FIFA World Cup, but their relationship continues to be strained. President Yoon Suk-yeol has expressed confidence that Japan-Korea relations will improve.

ISSUE 14 NORTH KOREA, CHINA, AND JAPAN

Vocabulary & Expressions:

get along with   *to have a friendly relationship with someone
- I always *get along with* my sister, but I usually argue a lot with my brother.

belligerent   *feeling or showing a readiness to fight or engage in war
- When I was a boy, there was a *belligerent* old man who lived down the street; he yelled angrily at anyone who walked past his house.

hostile   *acting with a spirit of opposition in feeling or action toward someone else
- The relations between North Korea and the United States have often been tense and *hostile* since the end of the Korean War.

short lived   *living or lasting for only a short time. Written as *short-lived* before a noun.
- My brother's relationship with his girlfriend was *short lived*; they broke up after only two weeks.

denuclearization   *to remove nuclear arms from a country
- In 1994, Ukraine agreed to begin the process of *denuclearization*.

endeavor   *to try hard; to make an effort
- My parents have a successful marriage because they always *endeavor* to understand and support each other.

deploy   *to arrange in a position of readiness, or to move to a strategic position
- The United States has *deployed* thousands of soldiers in Europe as part of NATO defenses.

THAAD   *Terminal High Altitude Area Defense, an American missile defense system designed to shoot down ballistic missiles
- *THAAD* has been deployed in the United Arab Emirates, Israel, Romania, and South Korea.

contain   *to prevent the expansion of a hostile power or political system
- After World War II, the US occupied both Germany and Japan in order to *contain* any future hostile actions by them.

rebound   *to recover from a setback, disappointment, or difficulty
- My cousin broke up with her boyfriend two months ago, but she seems to have *rebounded* now.

diplomatic   *relating to establishing and keeping good relations between the governments of different countries
- China did not establish *diplomatic* relations with the Republic of Korea until 1992.

strained   *not friendly or relaxed
- After Mary found out that her boyfriend had told a lie, their relationship became *strained*.

Open to Debate (1): 30 Korean Issues

Discussion Points:

1. Do you believe that North Korea is still a danger to South Korea? In what ways?
2. Would you like to visit North Korea? What areas and sites would you like to see?
3. Do you think South Korea is too dependent on China to buy Korean exports? How can Korea get more trading partners?
4. Would you like to visit China? What areas and sites would you like to see?
5. Why have South Korea and Japan continued to have difficult relations in spite of their 1965 treaty? Does Japan share all of the blame, or is South Korea also responsible?
6. Would you like to visit Japan? What areas and sites would you like to see?
7. What do you think will happen in the next 10 years between South Korea and North Korea? Between South Korea and China? Between South Korea and Japan?

Current Hot Topic: Dokto

The Dokto islands, AKA Takeshima or "Liancourt Rocks," lie in rich fishing grounds, 217 km from the east coast of Korea. The ownership of the islets has been disputed between Korea and Japan for decades. Both sides present historical arguments in favor of their ownership, though some historical documents seem unclear. In any case, Korea has had control of the islands since 1952, when the Korean Coast Guard occupied them. In 2012, Korea's president, Lee Myung-Bak, became the first Korean president to visit Dokto. Meanwhile, Japanese high school textbooks claim that Takeshima belongs to Japan, and Korea's occupation is illegal.

For Further Discussion:

1. Why can't Korea and Japan settle the issue of Dokto once and for all? It's clear that Korea has no intention of leaving the islands, so why doesn't Japan just give up their claims to the islands?
2. A few years ago, some Korean leaders proposed building hotels on the islands and turning them into a tourist resort. Do you agree with this idea?

I'm only motivated by money, and I'm running to achieve the world record for the 100-meter race because NIKE promised me billions of dollars as a bonus. With that money, I'll be able to retire ASAP and lead a cozy lifestyle for the rest of my life.

I'm self-motivated. I'm not running to make money, and I am determined to run until my last days. I just love running.

I'm able to run faster than both of them. I don't understand why NIKE hasn't tried to scout me. If they continue to ignore me, I will meet Adidas or Reebok next month.

● Topic Preview:

What part do sports play in your life? How often do you play sports? How often do you watch sports? Do you cheer enthusiastically for your country's team in international sports competitions? Do you feel a sense of pride when your country wins a lot of medals in the Olympics?

● Dialogue:

Linda: Hey, Mark, I just read that Miami will be one of the host cities for the 2026 World Cup.

Mark: Yeah, that's right. There are 16 host cities, in Canada, Mexico, and the US.

Linda: That's cool. Well, since you're from Miami, are you planning to attend any of the matches?

Mark: Oh, that's a long way off. I'm not sure where I will be at that time.

Linda: Well, you should try to get tickets when they're available, including a ticket for your good friend Linda.

Mark: Haha. I will see what I can do. I'm not a very nationalistic person, so I don't get too excited about cheering for any team. I say, "Let the best team win."

Linda: I see. Well, this World Cup will be the first one that will be hosted by three countries.

Mark: Yeah, that's true. Actually, it's surprising because nowadays many countries don't want to host international sports events because of the high cost of hosting.

Linda: Yeah, you're right about that, but it's an important event. You should try to go.

Mark: Okay. We can talk more about it as the time draws closer.

ISSUE-15

Obsession with Sports

In 1953, when South Korea emerged from the devastation of the Korean War, Koreans and their leaders were mostly concerned about survival. Sports took a back seat to the urgent task of reviving the national economy. When Syngman Rhee was president (1948–1960), the government was generally negative about promoting sports. However, when President Rhee sent the national soccer team to Japan in 1953 for the first match after decolonization, he admonished them by saying, "If you lose, throw yourselves into the border sea." Thus, sports in Korea were viewed as a political tool for gaining an advantage in international relations, a tendency known in academic circles as "sports nationalism."

President Park Chung-hee (1961–1979) is sometimes called "the father of modern sport in Korea." As a military officer, Park promoted sports as a development of the nation's fighting spirit. The government even used the slogan "Physical Fitness Is National Power" in an attempt to enhance the country's national prestige. Spurred by the success of the Tokyo Olympic Games in 1964, Korea built the National Training Center and established a procedure for the training of elite athletes.

During the presidencies of Chun Doo-hwan (1980–1988) and Roh Tae-woo (1988–1993), sport continued to be used as a tool for increasing Korea's international esteem. Chun promoted the slogan "the Establishment of a Sports Nation," and the country successfully hosted the 1988 Seoul Olympic Games. Korea won more medals than Japan, its archrival, and the notion of sports nationalism was elevated in Korea.

Subsequent national leaders have further served to cement sports nationalism into the nation's psyche. During the 2002 World Cup, when South Korea advanced to the semifinals, President Kim Dae-jung said proudly, "This was Korea's happiest day since Dangun—the god-king who, according to legend, founded the Korean nation."

ISSUE 15 OBSESSION WITH SPORTS

Vocabulary & Expressions:

devastation   *a situation involving almost complete destruction
- During World War II, much of Europe suffered incredible *devastation*.

take a back seat   *to have a less important position or status
- When Mr. Lee reached age 70, he was happy *to take a back seat* and let his son run the company.

revive   *to bring back to life, strength, freshness, or a healthy condition
- The new CEO was able to *revive* the old company and make it profitable again.

decolonization   *the act of freeing a people or area from being controlled by another country
- From 1945 to 1977, 50 African countries experienced *decolonization* from European powers.

admonish   *to give friendly advice or encouragement
- The teacher *admonished* her students to keep studying English and not give up.

prestige   *respect or admiration gained through success or excellence
- Doctors are usually regarded with *prestige* because of their years of medical study and hard work.

spurred   *inspired, stimulated, incited
- *Spurred* by the success of his restaurant, Mr. Kim decided to open two more restaurants.

elite   *representing the most the most gifted, skilled, or powerful members of a group
- Every country sends its *elite* athletes to the Olympics.

esteem   *a situation of favorable opinion, respect, or high regard
- Dr. Smith was held in high *esteem* by the entire town.

archrival   *a primary competitor
- Samsung and Apple are *archrivals* in the market for smartphones.

cement   *to make stronger
- Shared experiences, whether happy or sad, can truly *cement* a friendship.

psyche   *the soul, spirit, or personality of a person or group
- The nation's *psyche* was severely harmed when they lost the war.

Open to Debate (1): 30 Korean Issues

Discussion Points:

1. Why do you think Korea and Japan have continued to be rivals over so many generations, including in sports?
2. What sports does your country perform well in? What sports does it not do well in?
3. What are your favorite sports in the Winter Olympics? How about the Summer Olympics?
4. Have you ever watched an international sports event in person? What was the sport? Who won the game?

Read the following quotes about sports.
Can you explain what they mean? Do you agree with the idea expressed?

5. Winning isn't everything—but wanting to win is. Vince Lombardi
6. If you can't outplay them, outwork them. Ben Hogan
7. I've never lost a game. I just ran out of time. Michael Jordan

Current Hot Topic: Korean Women Golfers

In 1998, 20-year-old Korean golfer Pak Se-ri moved to the United States and joined the LPGA Tour full-time. She immediately found success and went on to win 22 events on the Tour before she retired in 2016. In 2007, at age 29, she qualified to join the World Golf Hall of Fame, becoming the youngest entrant ever. When she joined the LPGA, she was the only Korean player. Just 10 years later, there were 45 Koreans in the LPGA. *Golf World* writer Eric Adelson called Pak "a pioneer who changed the face of golf even more than Tiger Woods."

For Further Discussion:

1. Why have Korean women golfers become so incredibly successful on the LPGA Tour? Is their success based on genetics or just hard work?
2. Some people say that golf is a rich person's game. Do you think that's true? Why do so many businesspeople play golf?

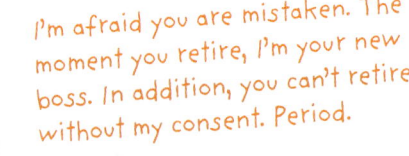

Topic Preview:

How do you feel when you see an elderly person still working? Do you feel sorry for them, or do you think that it's good that they're still able to work? Do you know anyone who is nearing retirement? Do you think they are prepared financially for retirement? How much monthly income do you think you'll need to have a comfortable retirement?

Dialogue:

Kimberly: Donald, how is your grandfather doing? He's in his 80s, right?

Donald: Yes, he's 85, and he's doing well. He's still teaching at the University of Texas.

Kimberly: Really? That's amazing! Doesn't he want to retire?

Donald: Not at all. He's been teaching for 55 years, and he still enjoys it.

Kimberly: And the US doesn't have forced retirement at a certain age?

Donald: No, that's impossible. This is America. Age discrimination is illegal. As long as you can do your job properly, you cannot be fired because of age.

Kimberly: Well, that's an admirable policy.

Donald: Yeah, I've even heard of teachers who are over age 100. However, there are a few jobs where they have forced retirement.

Kimberly: Really? What are those?

Donald: Mainly jobs that require high levels of physical and mental skill, such as military service, police officers, and commercial pilots.

Kimberly: I see. Well, that makes sense.

Planning for Retirement

Koreans are well known for having a strong work ethic. Like most people, they expect to enjoy a comfortable retirement. Unfortunately, the reality of retirement falls far short of that goal. A man named Mr. Oh is a case in point. After running his own tourism business for decades, Mr. Oh grew tired of the fierce competition and decided to retire at age 64. He quickly discovered that it was very difficult to survive on the national pension. He had no choice but to return to work. He saw a job advertisement for a position as a janitor and applied. He got the job, and now he hopes to work there for another 10 years.

Mr. Oh is just one of many retirees who are deciding to return to work, a phenomenon known as "unretirement." In most cases, these senior citizens need the extra money just to make ends meet. In fact, the employment rate for seniors aged 70 to 74 is about 33% in Korea, double the average among OECD countries. Unfortunately, working longer does not translate into affluence. Korea also has one of the highest rates of elderly poverty among OECD members. One report revealed that about 45% of elderly Koreans aged 65 or more were living below the poverty line.

Some experts say that the best way to prepare for retirement is to follow a philosophy known as FIRE. This acronym stands for "financial independence, retire early." Supporters of this approach say that it's possible to retire at age 45 or earlier if you make more money, save or invest 50% to 70% of your income, and spend as little as possible. Of course, these lofty goals will prove to be difficult for most people. Most Koreans believe that retiring at age 60 is an elusive dream.

ISSUE 16 PLANNING FOR RETIREMENT

Vocabulary & Expressions:

ethic
*an important moral principle. Not to be confused with *ethnic*, which refers to groups with common characteristics and customs.
- Respect for the elderly is an important *ethic* in many Asian countries.

fall short
*to fail to reach a goal or target
- Our national athletes hoped to win 20 gold medals in the Summer Olympics, but they *fell short* of that goal.

case in point
*an example or illustration of something
- Many Hollywood stars once held ordinary jobs; Harrison Ford, who worked as a carpenter, is a *case in point*.

fierce
*having great energy and enthusiasm
- Korea and Japan are always *fierce* competitors on the soccer field.

pension
*a sum of money paid each month to a person who has retired from work
- Most financial experts say that your *pension* should be about 75% of your preretirement income.

janitor
*a person who takes care of a building, such as a school or an office
- The *janitor* is responsible for taking out the trash and keeping the floors clean.

make ends meet
*to earn enough money to provide for basic needs
- If a person is earning less than $10 per hour, it's almost impossible to *make ends meet*.

translate into
*to lead to, result in
- The president claims that his tax cuts will *translate into* economic growth.

affluence
*the situation of having a lot of money and possessions
- Only people with *affluence* can live in Bayshore, Florida, because the homes are extremely expensive.

poverty line
*the minimum level of income that financial experts think is adequate; AKA *poverty limit*
- The *poverty line* for a married couple in the US is currently $21,770 per year.

acronym
*an abbreviation that is pronounced like a word, such as *NASA* or *UNESCO*
- Some people use the word *initialism* to refer to abbreviations where each letter is pronounced separately, as in *NBA*, and the word *acronym* to refer to abbreviations that are pronounced as words, as in *NATO*; however, other people use *initialism* and *acronym* with the same meaning.

lofty
*high ranking or admirable
- My sister has chosen the *lofty* goal of attending an Ivy League university.

elusive
*hard to find or capture
- The police still have not caught the *elusive* bank robber who robbed the local bank two years ago.

Open to Debate (1): 30 Korean Issues

Discussion Points:

1. Do you think the Korean national pension plan is adequate? If not, how could the government improve it?
2. Do you know anyone who is retired? Are they making ends meet, or do they work on a part-time job?
3. Do you think you can follow the FIRE approach so that you can retire early?
4. When would you like to retire? When do you think you'll be able to retire?

Read the following quotes about retirement.
Can you explain what they mean? Do you agree with the idea expressed?

5. You get old faster when you think about retirement. Toba Beta
6. Retirement is the only time in your life when time no longer equals money. Unknown
7. When a man retires, his wife gets twice the husband but only half the income. Chi Chi Rodriguez

Current Hot Topic: Forced Retirement

Korea is one of the most Confucian nations on Earth. An early missionary to Korea said, "Everyone in Korea is Confucian, including the Christians." One of the major beliefs of Confucianism is deep respect for parents, teachers, and the elderly. Age is associated with wisdom. In most Korean companies, it is rare for a younger worker to be promoted above an older worker. In spite of this long-held belief, Korea still engages in forced retirement in many professions. For example, college professors must retire by age 65. In a recent survey, 75% of Korean retirees said their retirement was forced.

For Further Discussion:

1. If we truly respect the elderly, shouldn't we allow them to keep working as long as they wish, without any forced retirement?
2. The most common reason cited for forced retirement is that elderly workers need to get out of the way to allow younger workers to be promoted. Do you think this argument is valid?

— People say you've become more beautiful recently. Did you have some cosmetic surgery?
— No, I've never even thought of going under the knife!
— What's the secret to your beauty then?
— I've been learning HOW TO SMILE more often and act more gracefully and cheerfully. That's all.
— Wow! That's a lot better than cosmetic surgery and free of charge, with no side effects. That's the best recipe for natural beauty I've ever heard.

Dog: Don't worry! Since we're not able to smile, we have no choice but to have some cosmetic surgery. Why don't you advertise your hospital to our friends? Your business will be booming once again.

Alas, our days are numbered! If people learn the recipe for natural beauty, we'll be out of business at once. I'm considering establishing an academy that trains people on how to smile.

Topic Preview:

Why would someone who is already beautiful want to have plastic surgery? Is it because of a lack of self-confidence? Why has Korea become "the plastic surgery capital of the world"? Do you agree with the old statement that "inner beauty is more important than outward beauty"? Who are your favorite Korean actors, actresses, and singers? Do you think any of them have had plastic surgery?

Dialogue:

Anthony: Karen, I need your advice.
Karen: Yeah? About what?
Anthony: Well, you know my girlfriend Carole.
Karen: Yes, of course. She's from Korea, right?
Anthony: Yeah, she is. Well, here's the problem: she wants to get plastic surgery, and she wants my approval and help.
Karen: She doesn't need plastic surgery! She's already beautiful.
Anthony: That's exactly what I said! But she wants to have some kind of surgery on her eyes. I think it's called "double-eyelid surgery."
Karen: Oh, I've heard of that. A lot of Korean women get that. They want to have Western-type eyelids.
Anthony: Well, I think it's totally unnecessary, but I don't want to be stubborn about it.
Karen: No, you shouldn't be stubborn. I think you should help her get what she wants.
Anthony: Really? Are you serious?
Karen: Yeah, I think you should go along with her wishes. You know that old saying: "happy wife, happy life," except in your case it's "happy girlfriend, happy life."
Anthony: Well, thanks very much for your advice. I'll think about it.
Karen: Don't mention it.

Plastic Surgery

The third Thursday in November is the day when Korean high school seniors take the College Scholastic Ability Test (CSAT), also known simply as the "college entrance exam." They have spent untold hours studying for the exam, and once it's over, they finally have time to pursue some leisure activities that they have postponed for years, such as traveling, getting their driver's license, and getting some plastic surgery. Non-Koreans will be surprised to find out that many Korean parents even pay for plastic surgery for their teenage children as a graduation gift. The most common procedures are the "double-eyelid surgery" and a "nose job."

According to a recent survey, about 90% of Koreans believe that a person's looks matter a lot in life. About two-thirds of Koreans say that having plastic surgery with the aim of getting a job or getting married is completely acceptable. Young women especially think that their looks are extremely important in a society where lookism prevails. Around 30% of women in their 20s have actually had plastic surgery. There have been many attempts to explain the ubiquity of plastic surgery in Korea. Some say that Confucianism has caused Korea to become an ultraconformist society, where everyone looks the same. Others say that Koreans want to look more "Western."

A multibillion dollar plastic surgery industry has arisen in Korea to serve not only Korean customers but also thousands of international customers. The Gangnam area of Seoul boasts about 500 cosmetic surgery centers that perform more than a million procedures per year. About half the patients come from other countries, especially from China. Plastic surgery patients account for about 20% of the million medical tourists who come to Korea. It is little wonder that South Korea has now been dubbed "the plastic surgery capital of the world."

ISSUE 17 PLASTIC SURGERY

Vocabulary & Expressions:

untold
*too great or too numerous to be counted
- Jeff Bezos, the founder of Amazon, has **untold** riches; he can buy anything that he wants.

plastic surgery
*a medical procedure that changes parts of the human body to improve its appearance; AKA *cosmetic surgery*
- *Plastic surgery* can be used to repair injured skin or simply to improve a person's attractiveness.

double-eyelid surgery
*a type of plastic surgery where the skin around the eye is reshaped to create an upper eyelid with a crease; medical term: *blepharoplasty*
- Korean women have **double-eyelid surgery** because they think double eyelids are more attractive than single eyelids.

nose job
*plastic surgery on the nose, usually for cosmetic purposes; medical term: *rhinoplasty*
- Lisa Kudrow, who starred on the popular sitcom *Friends*, admitted that she got a **nose job** while she was still in high school.

lookism
*discrimination based on a person's physical appearance
- Because of **lookism**, it's difficult in some cultures for overweight people to get a good job.

prevail
*to be usual, common, or widespread
- Expensive stores **prevail** in Beverly Hills, California.

ubiquity
*the situation of being everywhere at the same time
- The **ubiquity** of cell phones in the modern world means that people can always contact you.

Confucianism
*the system of ethics, education, and social relations taught by Confucius and his disciples
- **Confucianism** emphasizes many moral values, especially respect for one's parents and ancestors.

ultraconformist
*describing a person or society that follows very carefully the attitudes and behavior of the group to which they belong
- My dad works for an **ultraconformist** company; all the men wear a white shirt and dark tie every day.

boast
*to have something that you're proud of
- The City of Seoul **boasts** one of the top subway systems in the world.

little wonder
*not surprising
- I was bad at math in school; it's **little wonder** that I have trouble filling out tax forms.

dubbed
*to be called by a certain nickname
- Elvis Presley was **dubbed** "the king of Rock 'n' Roll."

Open to Debate (1): 30 Korean Issues

● ● ● ● *Open to Debate (1): 30 Korean Issues*

● **Discussion Points:**

1. In your opinion, what are the main reasons that so many Koreans choose to get plastic surgery?

2. Do you know anyone who has gotten plastic surgery? Do you think the surgery improved their looks?

3. Have you heard any stories about plastic surgery that failed? What happened?

4. Would you ever consider getting plastic surgery? What procedures would you want done?

Read the following quotes about plastic surgery.
Can you explain what they mean? Do you agree with the idea expressed?

5. I definitely believe in plastic surgery. I don't want to be an old hag. There's no fun in that. Scarlett Johansson

6. Nothing makes you look older than attempting to look young. Karl Lagerfeld

7. Plastic surgery is a postmodern veil. Nawal El Saadawi

● **Current Hot Topic: Plastic Surgery and the Entertainment Industry**

It seems that plastic surgery is taking over the entertainment industry in Korea. The group that receives the most plastic surgery is young people who are training to be idol singers. It appears that 90% of these idol trainees have had plastic surgery. The most common procedures are facial shaping and fat removal. One young woman dropped out of training after she was told by an agent, "Your nose is too high. You will need some surgeries, at least 10, maybe up to 20." Many medical experts express concern about plastic surgery on young people because they are still growing.

● **For Further Discussion:**

1. Who are your favorite Korean idol singers? Do you think they've had plastic surgery? Can you think of any famous singers who have never had plastic surgery?

2. If your son or daughter wanted to become an idol singer, would you approve of their dream even if it meant having numerous plastic surgeries?

We're making a living by selling drugs to the police. They're big customers for us.

We're making a living now by taking bribes from the gangsters because the government can't afford to pay us anymore.
No business, except the drug cartels, has survived due to the rampant crimes. We admit there's a symbiosis between the gangs and us.

In this crime-ridden country, we have no choice but to join the Mafia and live as their soldiers. Every job has evaporated because of the war between law enforcement officers and the drug cartels.

Topic Preview:

Do you think the crime rate is rising in your country? What types of crimes are increasing? Are there any types of crimes that are decreasing? Do you think the punishment for crime is strong enough in your country?

Dialogue:

Jessica: Hey Matthew, do they still have the death penalty in New Zealand?

Matthew: You must be kidding. The last execution of a criminal took place in 1957.

Jessica: Oh, I had no idea. What were the circumstances?

Matthew: A man named Walter Bolton was hanged after being found guilty of poisoning his wife.

Jessica: Oh, that's terrible!

Matthew: Well, personally, I think life in prison would have been a better sentence for him.

Jessica: Why do you say that?

Matthew: Well, he would have had to think about his crime every day for the rest of his life. I think that's punishment enough.

Jessica: I see your point. Well, I'm from Texas, and we certainly have a lot of executions.

Matthew: I heard that. Isn't Texas number one for executions in the US?

Jessica: You are correct. Texas has executed more than 500 prisoners since 1976.

Matthew: Wow! That's incredible.

Jessica: Yeah, it's really sad.

Rising Crime Rate

In September 2021, a 34-year-old Korean man living in Yeosu was fed up with the noise from his upstairs neighbors. He had complained to them before but to no avail. One night, he could stand the noise no longer. He went up to the neighbor's apartment around 12:30 am to confront them once again. An argument ensued, and he killed the couple, who were in their 40s, as well as injuring their elderly parents. Right after the crime, he went to the local police station and turned himself in. The number of floor noise complaints reported to Korean authorities has increased dramatically in recent years.

Since the 2000s, the domestic manufacturing of illegal drugs in Korea has plummeted. That seems like good news, except for the fact that Korea's illegal drug industry is now flourishing on the dark web. In 2021, Korean drug investigators busted the operators of the "Telegram Drug Room," a drug-trading social media chat room. Police were able to identify the culprit, who turned out to be an 18-year-old high school student. He used the room to connect with cargo ships that brought methamphetamines, ecstasy, and cannabis into Korea. Statistics show that the number of Koreans in their 20s arrested for drug offenses has increased by seven times in the last decade.

Each year, the US State Department publishes the *Trafficking in Persons Report*, which ranks governments based on their perceived efforts to combat human trafficking. Each country is placed into one of three tiers, with tier 1 being the best and 3 being the worst. In 2022, after being in tier 1 for many years, South Korea was downgraded to tier 2. The report cited concerns about the lack of serious efforts to protect victims of human trafficking, including forced labor victims in the fishing industry.

ISSUE 18 RISING CRIME RATE

Vocabulary & Expressions:

fed up
*unable or willing to endure a person or situation any longer
- Last week, my uncle got fed *up with* his job and just quit.

to no avail
*without success
- I tried to get an A⁺ in math class *to no avail*.

turn oneself in
*to bring yourself voluntarily to an authority, usually because you've done something wrong
- The student felt guilty about cheating and *turned himself in* to the teacher.

flourishing
*growing vigorously, actively, and successfully; thriving
- My uncle owns a *flourishing* clothing store on Main Street; it's very popular with young people.

bust
*to place under arrest
- Last week, two drug dealers were *busted* for selling meth.

culprit
*the person guilty of a crime or a fault
- The *culprit* expressed regret for his crimes.

methamphetamine
*a powerful synthetic drug that stimulates the central nervous system; AKA *meth*
- The production, sale, and possession of *methamphetamine* is banned in many countries.

ecstasy
*a synthetic mood-enhancing synthetic drug; chemical name: MDMA
- *Ecstasy* was banned in the United States in 1985.

cannabis
*a drug obtained from the dried leaves and flowers of the hemp plant; AKA *marijuana*
- *Cannabis* is legal in some American states but illegal in others.

perceived
*describing what seems to be true or apparent
- Most citizens are not satisfied with the government's *perceived* efforts to lower inflation.

tier
*a row, rank, layer, or level, usually arranged in a series one above the other
- The top *tier* of the English football league system is known as the Premier League.

downgrade
*to lower in grade, rank, position, or standing
- Because Susan often came to work late, she was *downgraded* from manager to assistant manager.

● ● ● ● Open to Debate (1): *30 Korean Issues*

● **Discussion Points:**

1. Why would someone murder their neighbors simply because of a noise complaint? What sort of prison sentence should this man receive?
2. Have you ever had to deal with noisy neighbors? How did you handle the situation?
3. Have you read about any celebrities who were caught taking illegal drugs? What happened?
4. If someone in your city wanted to buy illegal drugs, where would they go?
5. What can Korea do to improve their handling of human trafficking cases?

Read the following quotes about crime.
Can you explain what they mean? Do you agree with the idea expressed?

6. There's a simple way to solve the crime problem: obey the law; punish those who do not. Unknown
7. Don't do the crime if you can't do the time. Unknown
8. He who wishes to be rich in a day will be hanged in a year.
   Leonardo da Vinci

● **Current Hot Topic:** **The Death Penalty**

In 2021, Netflix released a new series entitled *The Raincoat Killer*. The three-part documentary details the horrific crimes of serial killer Yoo Young-chul. In the early 2000s, Yoo terrorized Korea with numerous murders of wealthy women and prostitutes. He was arrested in 2004 and sentenced to death for the murders of 20 people. Almost two decades later, Yoo still sits on death row at the Seoul Detention Center. The release of the Netflix series has prompted many Koreans to call for a stricter use of the death penalty. Meanwhile, religious groups are calling for the end of the death penalty.

● **For Further Discussion:**

1. Do you support the use of the death penalty? What sort of crimes should the death penalty be used for?
2. What are the best arguments against the death penalty? Do you think the EU was wise to prohibit the death penalty?

— You're gaining some weight these days, aren't you?
— It's true. But I don't know why. I just enjoy my simple hobbies: eating some fast food while watching TV or playing with my smartphone on my couch.
— Don't you know your current weight is the direct result of your hobbies? Why don't you try walking? It might help you shed your weight.
— I tried it. But the problem is that I'm always hungrier after taking a walk.

I don't eat fast food or watch TV. I have no smartphone to play with and no couch to lie down on. I don't know why I'm getting fatter too. I suspect that worrying about his obesity gives me lots of stress. My vet once told me that stress is the worst enemy you face while trying to control somebody's weight. I'll start worrying about my weight instead of worrying about his body.

Topic Preview:

Do you think your country has a problem with rising obesity? What do you think are the causes? Have you ever gone on a diet? Did you lose the weight that you wanted to lose? Did you keep the weight off? What do you think when you see an overweight person? Do you feel sorry for them?

Dialogue:

Daniel: Jennifer, I have a big problem!

Jennifer: What kind of problem do you have?

Daniel: I put on three kilograms during the pandemic! What am I going to do?

Jennifer: Well, that happened to a lot of people. We were all stuck inside.

Daniel: What about you? Did you gain any weight?

Jennifer: I think I gained one kilo, but as soon as my health club opened again, I started going several times a week.

Daniel: I see. I guess you lost the weight?

Jennifer: Yeah, after a couple of weeks I lost the weight. I also ate a lot of salads.

Daniel: Well, I think I need to join your health club. When are you going again?

Jennifer: As a matter of fact, I'm going this afternoon. Would you like to join me?

Daniel: Sure. Count me in.

Rising Obesity

A recent study conducted by the Korean Agency for Technology and Standards reveals that Koreans have grown around 5-6 cm taller over the last 40 years. Men increased in height by about 6.4 cm and women by 5.3 cm. The average height of Korean men is now 172.5 cm, and among women it is 159.6 cm. Most people think it's better to be taller, so the increased height could be viewed as a positive outcome.

Unfortunately not all of the results of the study were so positive. The study also concluded that the average body mass index (BMI) of Korean men is now about 25, indicating that almost 50% of Korean men are now considered obese. To accommodate the rising obesity of Koreans, the width of seats in the cinema has increased from 48 cm in the 1960s to 55 cm today. Likewise, subway seats have been expanded from 43.5 cm in the 1970s to 48 cm today. The research also concluded that the leg-to-body ratio of Koreans is becoming longer, meaning that Koreans' body shape is becoming more westernized.

The problem of rising obesity was only exacerbated by the COVID-19 pandemic. Levels of physical activity declined, and the prevalence of chronic diseases, such as obesity and diabetes, escalated. Strict rules of social distancing, the loss of active daily routines, the closure of health clubs, and the necessity to work from home have all combined to increase obesity. Nowadays, you can see many Koreans who are chubby or even have a muffin top.

Rising obesity among Korean children has been recognized as a major health problem for a long time. The situation became worse during the pandemic, as kids stayed home with their eyes glued to a computer screen. They also ate more fast food, brought by neighborhood delivery services.

ISSUE 19 RISING OBESITY

Vocabulary & Expressions:

outcome   *a result, consequence, or conclusion
- Our soccer team won in the final minute, so we were very happy with the *outcome* of the game.

body mass index *a measure of someone's weight in relation to height, using the formula BMI = weight (kg) / height (m)^2
- My weight is 75 kg, and my height is 1.75 m, so my *BMI* is 24.49 (75/1.75 × 1.75 = 75/3.0625 = 24.49).

obese   *very fat or overweight; noun form = *obesity*
- A person is considered *obese* when their weight is 20% or more above normal weight.

accommodate   *to make extra space or room for something
- The classroom was remodeled to *accommodate* 40 students instead of 25.

westernize   *to influence someone or something with ideas, customs, practices, or qualities that are associated with Europe and America
- Hollywood movies have *westernized* the thinking of many people around the world.

exacerbate   *to increase the severity, bitterness, or violence of something; to make something worse
- The town's many problems were *exacerbated* by the heavy rains.

prevalence   *the situation where something is happening, accepted, or practiced over a wide area
- Due to the *prevalence* of COVID-19, the government ordered all health clubs to close.

escalate   *to increase in intensity, extent, volume, number, or amount
- Fuel prices have *escalated* since the war started.

chubby   *somewhat fat; a little fat
- I was *chubby* in high school, but I lost weight, and now I'm thin.

muffin top   *slang for a roll of excess fat that hangs over a person's waist; AKA *a spare tire*
- My brother gained a *muffin top* during the pandemic, so he's going on a diet.

glued to   *watching something very closely for a long time
- You shouldn't keep your eyes *glued to* the TV; get out and do some exercise!

Open to Debate (1): 30 Korean Issues

Discussion Points:

1. Do you agree that it's a good thing to be tall? What advantages do tall people have?
2. Have you ever had your BMI checked? Were you satisfied with the results?
3. Did you gain any weight during the COVID-19 pandemic? Do you still have that extra weight or have you lost it?
4. What should schools and parents do to ensure that children get enough exercise?

Read the following quotes about obesity.
Can you explain what they mean? Do you agree with the idea expressed?

5. Obesity affects every aspect of people's lives, from health to relationships. Jane Velez-Mitchell
6. Obesity is a mental state, a disease brought on by boredom and disappointment. Cyril Connolly
7. Those who do not find time for exercise will have to find time for illness. Edward Stanley

Current Hot Topic: The Cause of Rising Obesity

Expats living in Korea are surprised to hear that many Koreans blame Western food for their country's rising obesity. Koreans often say that the influx of Western eating places like McDonald's, Baskin-Robbins, and Dunkin' Donuts are the main culprits for surging rates of obesity. However, it is helpful to point out politely that Koreans routinely eat large amounts of high-calorie, homegrown foods, such as grilled pork belly (*samgyeopsal*), fried chicken and beer (*chimaek*), fried street foods, and ramyun. Indeed, Korea is the number one consumer of ramyun worldwide. Also, the average adult Korean drinks about 90 bottles of soju annually.

For Further Discussion:

1. How often do you eat the high-calorie Korean foods mentioned in the reading passage? What are your favorites?
2. Studies of McDonald's customers reveal that the average McDonald's customer eats there three times per month. Even dedicated McDonald's lovers eat there only five times per month. Why do people, both Americans and Koreans, continue to blame McDonald's for widespread obesity?

— Have you ever been the victim of a scam?
— No, I've never been the victim of a scam in my life because I'm not interested in worldly affairs, such as money or fame. Don't you know that curiosity is what pulls people into scams?
— Wow! I envy you. By the way, what happened to your wife? Didn't you just marry her last month?
— She left her two kids with me and eloped with a young man two weeks after we got married.

I'm waiting for her because she promised that she would come back ASAP.

This might be the first time for my friend to be the victim of a love scam.

Dad, where's Mom?

Dad, I'm starving! Give me some food now!

🟢 Topic Preview:

Do you think your bank account is secure today? What steps does your bank take to keep your money safe? Do they use "multifactor authentication," where you must enter a code sent to your cell phone? Has anyone ever tried to hack your bank account or credit card? What happened?

🟡 Dialogue:

Lily: Adam, you won't believe what happened to me yesterday!

Adam: What happened?

Lily: I got a text message from my sister. She said she had been arrested and needed me to send her $2,000, so she could pay a fine and get out of jail.

Adam: Oh, that's terrible! What did you do?

Lily: Well, at first I thought it might really be true because she's on vacation now at a Mexican resort.

Adam: Well, did you send the money?

Lily: No, I got suspicious because the text message had several misspelled words, and my sister is very careful about spelling.

Adam: So the message turned out to be fake?

Lily: Yeah, it did. I called my mom, and she said she had just talked to my sister an hour before, and everything was fine.

Adam: Well, you were smart to double-check everything.

Lily: Yeah, I was almost the victim of a phishing attack.

Sexual Harassment

Tarana Burke is a survivor of sexual violence. She was sexually assaulted both as a child and a teenager. Her mother did her best to help Tarana's recovery and to encourage her to help others. While still a teenager, Tarana became an activist, helping girls with similar experiences and organizing protests against injustice. In 2006, she began to use the phrase "Me Too" in order to raise awareness of the pervasiveness of sexual assault in society. In 2017, actress Alyssa Milano began using #MeToo as a hashtag, and the phrase quickly went viral and developed into an international movement.

On January 29, 2018, the #MeToo movement came to Korea when prosecutor Seo Ji-hyun posted a message on the prosecution's internal network. She stated that she had been a victim of sexual harassment, and a week later she provided explicit details on JTBC's *Newsroom*. She was at a funeral in 2010 when an officer from the prosecutor's office touched her in a sexual way. She was so shocked by the perpetrator's behavior that she didn't know what to do. Later, she wondered if she had been suffering a hallucination. Eight years later, she mustered the courage to speak out, and other women soon joined her.

In February 2018, a young woman accused Cho Min Ki, a professor of theater at Cheongju University, of sexually harassing female students for years. Cho denied the accusation, calling it a baseless rumor, but then actor Song Ha-neul came forward and said the charges were true. On March 9, Cho was found dead at his home of an apparent suicide. Actor Cho Jae-hyun was also accused of sexual harassment. To his credit, he apologized and said, "I lived wrongly and acted wrongly. I am a sinner. I bow my head and apologize to the victims."

ISSUE 21 SEXUAL HARASSMENT

Vocabulary & Expressions:

activist — *a person who uses strong actions, such as public protests, to support one side of a controversial issue
- Yesterday, there were more than 10,000 anti-war *activists* in the streets protesting the war.

go viral — *to spread quickly and widely, especially by means of social media
- Ed Sheeran's song "Shape of You" was released in early 2017, and it quickly *went viral*.

explicit — *so clearly spoken or described that there is no doubt about the meaning
- I have the best math teacher; she always gives *explicit* instructions that are easy to understand.

perpetrator — *the person who committed a crime or offense; AKA *perp*
- The local bank was robbed last week, and the police are still looking for the *perpetrator*.

hallucination — *an experience of seeing objects or having experiences that are not real; a false belief or impression
- The doctors gave my grandfather so much medicine for his illness that he started having *hallucinations*.

muster — *to find, raise, gather
- My brother was afraid of his boss, but finally he *mustered* the courage to ask for a raise in salary.

speak out — *to tell about one's experiences or to state one's opinions boldly and bravely
- Because of the #MeToo movement, many women are now *speaking out* about their experiences.

baseless — *without supporting evidence; not based on fact; groundless
- The losing politician made many *baseless* claims that the election was stolen.

come forward — *to make the effort required to make a claim, provide information, volunteer, etc.
- Women who are victims of sexual harassment are often afraid to *come forward*.

apparent — *appearing to be real or true
- Smith is the *apparent* winner of the election, but we are still waiting for the official results.

to one's credit — *a phrase used to acknowledge that a person deserves some praise for doing a positive or honorable thing
- After the bank robber was arrested, *to his credit*, he told the police where the money was hidden.

sinner — *a person who breaks God's laws
- "I am not a saint, unless you think of a saint as a *sinner* who keeps on trying." Nelson Mandela

Open to Debate (1): 30 Korean Issues

Discussion Points:

1. Why is the entertainment industry the place of so much sexual harassment and assault?
2. If someone is found guilty of sexual harassment, what sort of punishment should they receive?
3. Can you think of any other Korean celebrities who have come forward with charges of sexual harassment? What happened?
4. Do you personally know anyone who experienced sexual harassment? What happened?
5. Can women also be guilty of sexual harassment? Do you know of any examples?

Read the following quotes about sexual harassment.
Can you explain what they mean? Do you agree with the idea expressed?

6. We should not use the term "harassment." What is happening today is sexual terrorism. Unknown
7. We must send a message across the world that there is no disgrace in being a survivor of sexual violence. The shame is on the aggressor. Angelina Jolie

Current Hot Topic: Sexual Assault in Sports

At age 6, Shim Suk-hee started short-track speed skating as a hobby. It was obvious from the start that Shim had an immense talent for the sport. She joined the Korean national team at age 15 and has now won several Olympic medals. The nation was shocked in January 2019 when Shim revealed that she was sexually abused while still a teenager by former coach Cho Jae-beom. Cho denied the accusation of sexual abuse but admitted that he had committed verbal and physical abuse as "discipline." A court did not agree and sent him to prison for 10.5 years.

For Further Discussion:

1. Do you think the prison sentence given to Cho was adequate? How many years in prison should he have gotten?
2. How can sexual harassment and assault of sports stars be prevented? If your daughter entered sports competitions, how would you ensure that she stayed safe?

Smartphones have replaced your camera, calendar, and your alarm clock. Furthermore, they're replacing your family because you hug them more often and spend more time with them until you get to sleep. There must be a time coming when we're going to marry smartphones. They can talk, shop, do chores, wash the dishes, and vacuum. They can easily play the role of a spouse.

I never dreamed that I would officiate such a strange wedding between a man and his smartphone. I'm afraid someday soon we'll be replaced by smartphones too.

I'm so angry that he's thinking about divorce at the exact moment we're marrying! He doesn't even know that we smartphones have progressed to the point that we're able to read his mind.

Today I'm marrying my smartphone. She can do everything I would expect a spouse to do. What's even better, a future divorce would be very easy, and I wouldn't have to pay any alimony.

Topic Preview:

Have you ever left your smartphone at home or misplaced it? How long did you have to go without using it? How did you feel? Do you think you could go a week without using your smartphone? If someone offered to pay you money not to use your smartphone for a month, how much would they have to pay you—$50, $100, $1,000, or more?

Dialogue:

Dorothy: Thomas, could I borrow your smartphone for a minute?

Thomas: Sure. What's the matter? Did you forget to bring your smartphone today?

Dorothy: No, I didn't actually. The problem is that my battery has completely died. It can no longer be recharged. I'm going to get a new battery later today.

Thomas: I see. Well, it's a good idea to have an extra battery just in case your first one dies.

Dorothy: Yeah, I agree with you about that. I'm going to buy two new batteries and keep them both charged up.

Thomas: That's a good idea. I feel so frustrated when I don't have access to my smartphone.

Dorothy: I know exactly what you mean. I just hope I don't get nomophobia.

Thomas: Nomophobia? What's that?

Dorothy: It means "a fear of not having your smartphone."

Thomas: I didn't know there was a word for that exact fear, but I think I have nomophobia. I'm always afraid of losing my smartphone or not having it with me.

Dorothy: I think we are in the same boat. We need to stop being so reliant on our smartphones!

Thomas: That's easier said than done.

Smartphone Addiction

When an American English teacher came to Korea to teach English in the mid-90s, he was amazed to see how many Koreans carried a beeper. In the United States, only physicians or firefighters carried beepers because they were on call 24-7. However, the English teacher observed Koreans from every walk of life who carried a beeper: teachers, students, office workers, homemakers, and so forth. It became clear that Koreans were dedicated aficionados of high-tech gadgets. Nowadays, Korea is one of the most wired countries in the world and a nation with one of the highest Internet speeds. Almost every citizen from preschoolers to grandparents has a smartphone.

Smartphones are wonderful devices for keeping in touch with family and friends, communicating with bosses and colleagues, obtaining help during emergencies, and finding information quickly. However, they pose some dangers. Frequent users of smartphones can quickly become addicted to them. According to a study conducted by the government, one out of three Korean students is too dependent on their smartphone and at risk of addiction and lower performance in school. Simply put, they spend too much time on their smartphones and show a lack of self-control in using them. They also suffer from nomophobia.

Korea's youth are not the only demographic that struggles with smartphone dependence. Another recent study concluded that 1 in 4 Koreans could be diagnosed with smartphone addiction. While youth aged between 10 and 19 had the highest percentage of addiction, even 17% of the elderly, aged 60 and older, were deemed to be too dependent on smartphones. In order to reduce the number of smartphone addicts, the Ministry of Science and ICT has established 18 Internet Addiction Prevention Centers across the country. Koreans can use the center's website to get an online diagnosis of smartphone addiction, as well as free counseling.

ISSUE 22 SMARTPHONE ADDICTION

Vocabulary & Expressions:

on call — *ready or available when and if needed
- My uncle is a firefighter; he's always *on call* unless he's on vacation.

walk of life — *a person's job or position in society
- The people at the meeting came from all *walks of life*—doctors, teachers, businesspeople, students, and so on.

homemaker — *a person who manages a household, especially as a spouse and parent
- Nowadays, many people prefer the word *homemaker* to the old-fashioned word *housewife*.

aficionado — *a person who is an enthusiastic fan or supporter of a certain thing, activity, or interest
- My mother is an *aficionado* of old movies.

gadget — *a small useful device that is often very interesting and sometimes unusual
- Drones are one of the most interesting *gadgets* in the modern age.

wired — *having an excellent working connection to the Internet
- Jackson Health System in Miami is one of the most *wired* hospitals in the US.

pose — *to create, produce, form, result in
- Mountain climbing always *poses* the risk of injury.

at risk — *in a dangerous situation or condition that may cause loss or injury
- Many elderly people are *at risk* of becoming victims of scams.

simply put — *in clear, direct, and easily understood words
- What is a cardiac arrest? *Simply put*, it's a heart attack.

nomophobia — *fear of being without one's cell phone
- The more we use our cell phones, the more likely we are to experience *nomophobia*.

demographic — *a specific part of a population having similar characteristics
- Most watchers of cable TV news are from the *demographic* of age 55 and older.

deem — *to consider, judge, or think
- Most parents *deem* it wise for their children to wait until they have a good job before they get married.

Open to Debate (1): 30 Korean Issues

Discussion Points:

1. We often see some people who own more than one smartphone. Why do you think they have multiple phones?
2. Why do Koreans love high-tech gadgets so much?
3. Do you know anyone who is addicted to their smartphone? What is their life like?
4. How many texts do you send each day? Who do you text mostly?
5. Have you ever experienced nomophobia? What happened?

Read the following quotes about smartphones.
Can you explain what they mean? Do you agree with the idea expressed?

6. Apparently, we love our own smartphones, but we hate everyone else's. Pay attention to people, not to your phone. Unknown
7. Life is what happens when your smartphone is charging. Unknown
8. The challenge for a human now is to be more interesting to another person than his or her smartphone. Alain de Botton
9. We take better care of our smartphone than ourselves. We know when the battery is depleted and recharge it. Arianna Huffington
10. When the phone was tied with a wire, humans were free. Unknown

Current Hot Topic: Computer Gaming Addiction

In 2005, a 28-year-old Korean man played the computer game Starcraft in an Internet café for 50 straight hours until he collapsed. Within a few hours he was dead. In 2011, the Korean government passed a "shutdown law" (AKA "Cinderella Law"), which banned computer gaming between midnight and 6:00 am. The law was replaced in 2021 with a "choice permit" system, which lets parents arrange approved playtimes. In 2019, Korea opened smartphone and gaming addiction treatment camps, which were also known as "Internet detox camps." The camps help addicts get involved in other healthy activities and build social connections.

For Further Discussion:

1. Some critics say that Korea's laws that control computer gaming are unrealistic and a violation of young people's rights. Do you agree with this opinion? What else could the government do to prevent gaming addiction?
2. Do you know anyone who seems addicted to computer games? What is their life like?

> Years ago, when I thought I was at the end of my rope, I tied a knot and hung on instead of choking my neck with the rope. Now I've become a world champion in CrossFit.

> Way to go!

> He's a great role model for me, but I still have no idea how to turn excuses for committing suicide into reasons for living. I'd better put my dangerous idea aside until tomorrow. When I wake up tomorrow morning, I hope some good ideas will pop into my head.

Topic Preview:

What causes people to commit suicide? Does your country have a suicide hotline? If you had a friend who was thinking about suicide, what advice would you give them? Can you think of any celebrities or politicians who committed suicide? What happened?

Dialogue:

Joseph: Hey, Donna. I just came across a new term. I wonder if you know what it means.

Donna: What term are you talking about?

Joseph: "The Werther effect."

Donna: Oh, the Werther effect? Are you reading Goethe's novel?

Joseph: No. What novel?

Donna: *The Sorrows of Young Werther.* That's where the term Werther effect comes from.

Joseph: No, I'm afraid I'm not as well read as you. I'm actually doing some research on suicide, and I came across this term.

Donna: Well, the Werther effect refers to copycat suicides.

Joseph: Oh, I see. You mean that if a well-publicized suicide occurs, some people may do the same thing.

Donna: That's right. When Marilyn Monroe took her life on August 4, 1962, there was an increase of 200 more suicides than average for that month. That's the Werther effect.

Joseph: I see. Thanks for the information. By the way, what happened to Young Werther?

Donna: I'm not going to say. You'll have to read the book to find out.

Joseph: Okay! I'll do it.

Suicide

The COVID-19 pandemic took many more lives than simply those who died of the disease. In late 2021, because of a resurgence of COVID-19 infections, the Korean government reinstated restrictions on the operation hours of restaurants, as well as on the number of people allowed inside. A man named Mr. Jung, a self-employed owner of a small Chinese restaurant, had struggled to keep his business afloat. With the reintroduction of severe COVID-19 rules, he saw no way out of his desperate financial bind and chose to end his life.

In June 2022, a man named Mr. Cho was in dire straits. The 36-year-old had invested more than 100 million Korean won ($77,000) in cryptocurrency, whose price had been tanking for months. He also owed 150 million won in credit card debt and loans. In his despair, Cho drove his car, accompanied by his wife and 10-year-old daughter, and plunged into the waters of Songgok Port in Wando, South Jeolla Province. All three family members died in what the media called a "family suicide."

In early 2021, a female Air Force sergeant named Lee was pressured by a male officer into attending a work dinner, despite COVID-19 restrictions on such gatherings. Three days after the dinner, she filed a complaint with the Air Force, alleging that the officer had groped her in the vehicle on the way home. When it seemed as though the Air Force's gender equality center was ignoring her complaint, Sergeant Lee took her own life. Later, the accused officer also took his own life.

The cases cited above are just a few shocking examples of the more than 13,000 Koreans who commit suicide each year. In fact, South Korea has had the highest suicide rate in the OECD every year since 2003, except for two years.

ISSUE 23 SUICIDE

Vocabulary & Expressions:

resurgence *a time when something starts to happen again; a renewal
- After the COVID-19 pandemic slowed, there was a **resurgence** of interest in travel.

reinstate *to place again in a former position or situation
- The employee was fired, but later he was **reinstated**.

afloat *free of major difficulties, especially financial difficulties
- My uncle opened a new store, and he worked hard to keep it **afloat**.

reintroduction *the process of making something exist, happen, or be used again as it was previously
- At my school, there has been a **reintroduction** of the old rule banning cell phones in the classroom.

no way out *no solution to a problem; no way to avoid a difficulty
- If you see **no way out** of a difficult situation, you should talk to a counselor, so you can find a solution.

bind *a difficult situation
- My brother said, "I'm in a real **bind**. Can you loan me $50?"

straits *situation of difficulty or distress
- The lost mountain climbers were in dire **straits**.

tank *to decline rapidly or do poorly; to fail
- People had great expectations for the 2019 film *Cats*, but it **tanked** during the first week.

despair *a complete loss of hope
- If your girlfriend breaks up with you, it's natural to feel **despair**, but better times will come.

plunge *to leap or dive suddenly
- The children **plunged** into the swimming pool to get the ball.

allege *to accuse someone of a crime
- The government **alleged** that the company had cheated its customers.

grope *to touch another person in a sexual manner without their consent
- The Tokyo Metro has special cars for women only, so they can avoid being **groped**.

Open to Debate (1): 30 Korean Issues

Discussion Points:

1. Korea has laws that allow bankruptcy, which frees a person from their debts, so why would anyone commit suicide because of financial problems?
2. Do you think the military takes cases of sexual assault seriously enough? What needs to change in the military culture?
3. Do you personally know someone who committed suicide? What happened?
4. What can the Korean government do to reduce the suicide rate?

Read the following quotes about suicide.
Can you explain what they mean? Do you agree with the idea expressed?

5. Suicide is a permanent solution to a temporary problem. Phil Donahue
6. Choosing to live is never easy, but it's always worth it. Unknown
7. He who has a "why" to live can bear almost any "how." Friedrich Nietzsche
8. When it is darkest, we can see the stars. Ralph Waldo Emerson
9. You are bigger than the sea you're sinking in. Katie Beth
10. Happiness is not by chance, but by choice. Jim Rohn

Current Hot Topic: Celebrity Suicides

In 2008, Journalist Kim Dae-o appeared on a TV entertainment program hosted by actor Ahn Jae-hwan. Ahn seemed nervous and was behaving oddly. He had a side business that was failing, and he had become the target of hateful online comments. Kim expressed her concern to an actress who was an old friend: "I am worried that Ahn might choose to end it all." The actress said that Ahn's friends were trying to help him. Later that month, Ahn took his own life. Forty days later, that actress, Choi Jin-sil, also took her life, apparently because of abusive Internet comments.

For Further Discussion:

1. Most people think that celebrities lead a wonderful and enchanting life. Why would a celebrity take their own life? Do you think it should be a crime to post online hateful comments?
2. Can you think of any other celebrities who have taken their own lives? What were the circumstances?

— You have beautiful tattoos!
— Thanks. I love these words: "Love Myself" and "Never Give Up." Do you have any tattoos?
— Yes, a lot!
— A lot? You don't seem to have any tattoos.
— They're in my mind. I don't think they should be on my skin.

I have lots of tattoos in my mind too. My favorite is "God loved the birds and invented trees. Man loved the birds and invented cages." I want to fly to God's land and live there!

Topic Preview:

Why do people get tattoos? What message are they trying to send to others by having a tattoo? Can you think of any actors or musicians who have tattoos? What kind of tattoos do they have? Can you think of any successful CEOs or businesspeople who have tattoos? Would you allow your teenage son or daughter to get a tattoo?

Dialogue:

Deborah: Hey, Richard. I heard you just spent a month in Korea.

Richard: Yeah, that's right. I was visiting a friend of mine who teaches English there.

Deborah: Wow! I envy you. Korea is such a cool country. Did you eat a lot of Korean food?

Richard: Of course. I enjoyed lots of *kimchi bokumbap*, *dolsot bibimbap*, *kalbi*, and many other foods.

Deborah: Nice! Did you do anything interesting?

Richard: I saw a lot of historical sites. I also got a tattoo.

Deborah: What? You got a tattoo? I thought that was illegal in Korea.

Richard: Well, it's illegal unless the tattoo artist is a licensed medical professional.

Deborah: And you got your tattoo from a licensed tattoo artist?

Richard: Actually, I didn't. I got one from a tattoo artist whose shop is hidden.

Deborah: Oh, my! Well, what kind of tattoo did you get? I don't see any tattoos on you.

Richard: I got a dragon tattooed on my upper arm. You want to see it?

Deborah: Yeah, sure. Pull up your sleeve….Well, it's very artistic and well done.

Richard: Thanks. Korea has a lot of great tattoo artists. It's just too bad they have to stay out of sight.

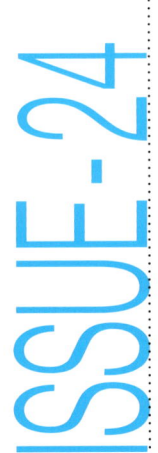

102 Open to Debate (1): 30 Korean Issues

Tattoo Artistry

If you have ever seen boy band sensation BTS perform on television, you probably noticed something bizarre about the appearance of Jungkook, the group's youngest member. He covers his arms and hands with long sleeves or tape. Why would a handsome young performer feel a need to do this? The reason is simple: the Korea Communications Commission (KCC) requires that broadcasters blur tattoos, and Jungkook has many tattoos on his arms and hands. Tattoos are legal in Korea, and displaying a tattoo is also legal. However, there is still a stigma against tattoos among many older people because tattoos have been traditionally associated with gangs and criminals. At the very least, they are still considered unprofessional by many business leaders.

In Korea, tattoos can only be done legally by a medical professional. Article 27 of the Korean Medical Service Act states that medical practices, including tattoos, can only be conducted by licensed medical personnel. From time to time, various politicians have tried to modernize the law. In mid-2021, Justice Party Rep. Ryu Ho-jeong drafted a bill that would liberalize tattooing. To drive her point home, she got several temporary tattoos applied to her own back and allowed the media to take pictures. Most young people supported her proposal, but they criticized Ryu for mentioning Jungkook to argue for her new law.

In spite of the strict requirements of Korean law, there are thousands of tattoo artists operating in Korea. They cannot advertise their business openly, so they rely on social media posts and referrals from satisfied customers. Some tattoo artists have become world famous, including an artist named Doy, who has inked Hollywood celebrities, including Brad Pitt, Lily Collins, and Steven Yeun. Those who regret getting a tattoo can always visit one of Korea's many laser tattoo removal clinics.

ISSUE 24 TATTOO ARTISTRY

Vocabulary & Expressions:

sensation — *a cause or object of much excitement and interest
- *Titanic* was the movie **sensation** of Hollywood in 1997.

bizarre — *very strange or odd
- The man in the coffee shop was behaving in a very **bizarre** manner.

blur — *to make unclear or hard to see
- If a driver's vision is **blurred** by fog, he should pull off the road until the fog clears.

stigma — *a mark of shame, disgrace, or dishonor
- Unfortunately, there is a **stigma** against people who were in prison, making it difficult for them to find a job.

unprofessional — *not showing a polite and careful businesslike manner in the workplace
- In most offices, it is considered **unprofessional** to wear shorts to work.

from time to time — *occasionally; once in a while
- I graduated from college 10 years ago, but I still like to visit the college **from time to time**.

draft — *to write the first version of a law, essay, or plan, which will later be revised
- After lawmakers **draft** a new law, they discuss it a lot before they write the final version.

liberalize — *to make more open minded and less strict
- Same-sex marriage was illegal in the US until 2015, when the Supreme Court **liberalized** the laws.

to drive one's point home — *to say something in a very strong or forceful way; also written as *drive home one's point*
- John raised his voice **to drive his point home** during the debate.

referral — *a recommendation to get treatment, help, information, or service from a certain person
- When I needed a doctor to perform some medical tests, I got a **referral** from my aunt.

ink — *to tattoo; to put a tattoo on someone
- Angelina Jolie has been **inked** more than 20 times, mostly with words and phrases from various languages.

regret — *to be sorry for; to wish you had not done a certain thing
- I **regretted** my decision to take a taxi on a Friday night because the traffic was heavy.

Open to Debate (1): 30 Korean Issues

Open to Debate (1): 30 Korean Issues

● Discussion Points:

1. Why do some Koreans still associate tattoos with gangsters and criminals?
2. It has been said that people get tattoos because they want to send the message that they are dangerous, powerful, and to be respected. Is there any truth to this claim?
3. Do you know anyone who got a tattoo? Do you know anyone who had a tattoo removed? Why did they want it removed?
4. Would you ever consider getting a tattoo? What kind of design would you choose?

Read the following quotes about tattoos.
Can you explain what they mean? Do you agree with the idea expressed?

5. Tattoos are permanent and a lifelong commitment, the same as marriage. Chester Bennington
6. My body is my journal, and my tattoos are my story. Johnny Depp
7. When all the people covered in tattoos turn about 70 years old, they're going to look like a strange race of melting clowns. Dana Gould

● Current Hot Topic: Who Should Perform Tattoos?

If you have a skin problem, you visit a dermatologist, a physician who specializes in diseases of the skin. If you want to enhance the beauty of your skin through cosmetic surgery, you visit a plastic surgeon. Why then would you allow a tattoo artist to pierce your skin with a needle? Korean physicians have used this type of argument for years in order to maintain legal control of tattooing. However, tattoo artists claim that tattooing is not a medical procedure but an artistic practice. They say they should be allowed to perform tattoos legally as a work of art.

● For Further Discussion:

1. Korean law currently agrees with the physicians and allows only licensed medical personnel to perform tattoos. Do you think this law should be changed so that tattoo artists can do their work legally?
2. If your children wanted to get a tattoo, would you allow them to do so? What about pierced ears (for earrings)? What about other types of piercings (nose ring, lip ring, etc.)?

— What happened? All the people have vanished. Where did they go?
— They have immigrated to the Republic of Seoul.
— What? Seoul was the capital city of Korea, wasn't it?
— That's right, but Korea has died out because people didn't like to live there any longer.
— Why not?
— In the Republic of Seoul, they can have access to well-developed mass transit and medical and recreational facilities. In addition, they can easily get a job and marry there.
— The Republic of Seoul is a paradise, isn't it? Let's go to Seoul! I want to get a job and remarry there!
— No way. They no longer accept ELDERLY immigrants like us.

Topic Preview:

If you had to choose three words to describe Seoul, what words would you choose? Do you think Seoul is too big and too overcrowded, or does its large size and population add to its charisma? What are the most famous sites in Seoul? Do you think the capital of Korea should remain in Seoul, or should it be moved to a central location in the country?

Dialogue:

David: Carol, I heard that you just returned from a visit to Seoul.

Carol: That's right. I was there for three weeks. I had so much fun.

David: Great! What was impressive about the city?

Carol: Well, it's a very modern city with an outstanding public transportation system, but it also has a lot of historic charm.

David: What historic sites did you visit?

Carol: I saw many of them, including Gyeongbok Palace, Insadong, and Dongdaemun.

David: I'm sure they were all fascinating.

Carol: Yes, everything was great, but I was shocked to find out that Korea is thinking about moving the capital out of Seoul to another city in the center of the country.

David: Wow! I can't believe that! Seoul is the most famous city in the country.

Carol: Of course, you're right. Seoul has been the capital since 1394. I cannot imagine another city taking the position of capital.

David: Well, I hope they think this matter through very carefully. Brazil tried to do the same thing back in the 1960s, and the change was not completely successful.

Carol: Yeah, I hope they keep Seoul as the capital. It's a huge city but charming at the same time.

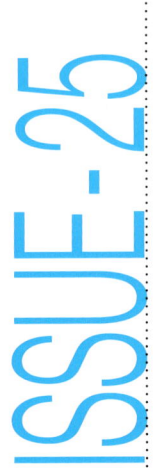

The Republic of Seoul

Seoul is the capital of the Republic of Korea and the largest city in the country. It is a much-loved city with accolades too numerous to mention. In 2015, Seoul was rated as Asia's most livable city with the second highest quality of life globally. The Seoul area is home to many world-famous companies, including Samsung, Hyundai, LG, and Kia, and the city exerts a major influence in global affairs. Seoul has hosted numerous major international events, including the 1986 Asian Games, 1988 Summer Olympics, and 2002 FIFA World Cup.

In spite of its inestimable value to the nation, Seoul has one major flaw: it is simply too big. The population of the city itself is approximately 10 million, but the greater metropolitan area has been growing steadily for many decades, while other areas of the country have been declining in population and influence. In 2020, for the first time, the population of the Seoul metropolitan area exceeded the population of the rest of the country. In other words, more than 50% of Koreans now live in Seoul or one of its surrounding cities.

When Roh Moo-hyun campaigned for president in 2002, he promised to move the capital of the country to a central location, to Sejong City, located 171 km south of Seoul. In his inaugural address, Roh said, "Decentralization of power to the provinces and balanced national development have become tasks that cannot be put off any longer." President Roh tried in earnest to move government offices to Sejong City, and he was partially successful because some ministries were moved to the city. However, in 2004, the Constitutional Court ruled that the capital must remain in Seoul. When Yoon Suk-yeol became president in 2022, he pledged to forge ahead with plans to relocate Korea's capital from Seoul.

ISSUE 25   THE REPUBLIC OF SEOUL

Vocabulary & Expressions:

too numerous to mention   *very many. Note: this idiom always comes after the noun it modifies.
- My parents have helped me in ways *too numerous to mention*.

livable   *suitable for living in; comfortable
- My uncle spent a lot of money remodeling an old house, but now it's very *livable*.

quality of life   *overall enjoyment of life; general well-being
- The new medical clinics have increased the *quality of life* for everyone in the city.

exert   *to use influence or authority forcefully or effectively
- The elderly senator was retired, but he still *exerted* a lot of influence in Washington.

inestimable   *too valuable or excellent to be measured; priceless
- The museum is full of ancient items of *inestimable* value.

flaw   *a small weakness or fault
- The price of the smartphone was marked down because it had a *flaw* on the front, a small scratch.

metropolitan   *relating to a large city, including its surrounding suburbs and neighboring communities
- The population of Los Angeles is about 4 million, but the population of the *metropolitan* area is more than 13 million.

decentralization   *the change of power and control from a central authority to regional and local authorities
- The new president promised to begin the *decentralization* of the control of education from the national level to the local level.

put off   *to delay or postpone
- My teacher has been sick, so our midterm exam has been *put off* for two weeks.

in earnest   *with serious or sincere intent
- Many college graduates search for a job *in earnest* but still find it difficult to get a job.

forge ahead   *to move forward slowly but steadily
- We *forged ahead* through the storm until we reached home.

Open to Debate (1): *30 Korean Issues*

Discussion Points:

1. Why do some Korean politicians want to move the capital to Sejong City? What are the pros and cons of this move?
2. "Seoul Citizens Day" has been held every October since 1994, when Seoul celebrated its 600th year as the capital of Korea. How would you feel if this famous city was required to give up its honored position as the nation's capital? Would it be a sad day for Korea?
3. What are the most memorable events that you have attended in Seoul?
4. Why do so many people flock to Seoul? Do you want to live in Seoul too? Why or why not?

Read the following quotes about Seoul.
Can you explain what they mean? Do you agree with the idea expressed?

5. Regional governments must struggle and beg to secure funding. Seoul, on the other hand, almost effortlessly receives more than enough funding and support from the central government. Wan-ju Kim, Mayor of Jeonju, 2004
6. The job of Seoul mayor is as important as that of president.
   Chung Mong-joon
7. Seoul, Up and Running Again for Fairness. The new city slogan of Seoul, 2021.

Current Hot Topic: Sejong City: Korea's Brasília?

In 1960, Brazil moved its capital from Rio de Janeiro to Brasília, a planned city created to become the new capital. While the city has won awards for its modern architecture and artistic planning, *Forbes* called Brasília an "office campus" that has no hopes of becoming a normal city. According to Yum Tae-jung, a journalist with the *JoongAng Ilbo*, the same thing may be happening with Sejong City. When Yum visited Sejong City in 2020, he observed a city still under construction and lacking practical infrastructure. In Yum's words, Sejong City was "bustling yet desolate, all at the same time."

For Further Discussion:

1. Do you think Sejong City will become like Brasília? Would you like to live in Sejong City? How much annual salary would it take to convince you to move there?
2. Pelé, the world-famous footballer, described Brasília as follows: "When I was a footballer, I surrounded myself with footballers. We were all friends. But in Brasília you don't know who your friends are. It can be a dangerous place." What do you think Pelé meant? Do you think Sejong City will become a place with no friends?

Topic Preview:

What are the hardest jobs in your country? What are the easiest jobs? Who is the hardest working person that you know? What is their life like? Do you know anyone who died of working too hard? What happened?

Dialogue:

Betty: John, I heard you got a new job with United Parcel Service.

John: Yeah, that's right. I just finished my first week.

Betty: Well, how was it? Did you enjoy the work?

John: Well, I'm still learning, but I'm surprised at how many hours I had to work.

Betty: Really? I thought UPS drivers worked an eight-hour day.

John: Some days are eight hours, but lately I've worked 10 to 12 hours on some days.

Betty: Wow! That's a lot. Do you get overtime pay?

John: Yes, I do if I work more than 40 hours per week, but I don't really want to work overtime.

Betty: No? Why not?

John: I think 40 hours per week is enough. It's important to balance work and leisure time. I want to spend time with my wife and kids.

Betty: Yeah, I see what you mean. Don't let overwork destroy your health.

John: You can say that again.

Too Much Work

In late 2020, a 36-year-old Korean delivery worker named Kim Duk-yeon was exhausted. He had just worked a 21-hour shift, delivering more than 400 packages during the height of the COVID-19 pandemic. Now it was an hour before sunrise and almost time to begin another shift. He texted a supervisor, asking for permission to skip a round of parcel deliveries. He wrote, "It's too much. I just can't." Four days later, Mr. Kim was dead.

Another delivery driver, 27-year-old Jang Deok-jin, met a similar fate. He was a Taekwondo enthusiast who lost 15 kg after working 18 months of night shifts. One morning, he came home from finishing his tedious night shift and went into the bathroom to take a shower. His father found him dead in the bathtub an hour later. His grieving father blamed himself for not discouraging his son from working so hard. However, the elder Jang took his anger to Korea's National Assembly. He begged a group of congressmen to look into the circumstances of his son's death.

Jang's plea got the attention of President Moon Jae-in, who called for an immediate improvement of the working conditions endured by delivery workers. As it turned out, Kim and Jang were two of 16 delivery workers who died in 2020. The families of these workers described the cause of their deaths with one Korean word: *gwarosa*. This term is used to describe a sudden death due to heart failure or stroke caused by excessive hard work.

In response to President Moon's concern, the Ministry of Employment and Labor urged Korea's logistics companies to commit to an overhaul of their inhumane working conditions. Three of the biggest firms pledged to reduce the workload of their staff, but it remains to be seen how much improvement will actually occur.

ISSUE 26 TOO MUCH WORK

Vocabulary & Expressions:

round
*a series or cycle of repeated actions or events
- I admire bus drivers because they make the same daily **round** without becoming too bored.

meet one's fate
*to die; also used in expressions like *meet a similar fate, meet the same fate*, etc.
- In the film *Skyfall* (2012), Raoul Silva **meets his fate** at the hands of James Bond; Lyutsifer Safin **meets a similar fate** in *No Time to Die* (2021).

enthusiast
*a person who is very excited about something
- My father is a true World Cup **enthusiast**.

tedious
*tiring because of length or boredom
- Computer programming seems like such a **tedious** job to me, but some people like it.

look into
*to investigate, study, or analyze
- The police are **looking into** the cause of the car accident.

turn out
*to prove to be; to come to be; to end up
- I hoped to get an A⁺ in English class, but as it **turned out**, I got a B⁺.

stroke
*a sudden serious illness caused by lack of oxygen to the brain
- Signs of a **stroke** include sudden weakness in the face, arm, or leg, especially on one side of the body.

logistics
*management of the flow of things from the point of origin to the customer
- The **logistics** of getting millions of packages from Amazon to their customers requires thousands of delivery workers.

overhaul
*to examine thoroughly and make necessary changes and improvements
- The program to help the elderly is not doing a good job; it needs to be completely **overhauled**.

inhumane
*not showing kindness and sympathy for people or animals
- The Humane Society opposes any **inhumane** treatment of animals.

pledge
*to promise seriously to take a certain action
- President Obama **pledged** to support Joe Biden as the next president.

remain to be seen
*describing a situation whose outcome is not exactly known or decided; to be uncertain
- France has a great soccer team, but it **remains to be seen** if they can win the next FIFA World Cup.

●●●● Open to Debate (1): 30 Korean Issues

Discussion Points:

1. Korea is known as a "hurry-hurry" (*ppalli ppalli*) culture. What are the pros and cons of this type of work ethic?
2. Do you think the companies that worked their delivery drivers to death should be required to make a financial payment to the workers' families? What is a reasonable amount?
3. Did you get more home deliveries during the pandemic? What kinds of products did you order?
4. Have you ever had a job where the work was too hard or too long? What happened?

Read the following quotes about work.
Can you explain what they mean? Do you agree with the idea expressed?

5. The only effective answer to organized greed is organized labor.
   Thomas Donahue
6. People should work to live, not live to work. Unknown
7. It is not work that kills, but no work and overwork. Aldus Manutius

● **Current Hot Topic:** Too Little Sleep

A 29-year-old public relations officer named Ji-Eun did not want to become a workaholic, but she had no choice. She normally worked from 7:00 am to 10:00 pm, but sometimes she worked until 3:00 am. Her boss would often call in the middle of the night, requesting some work to be done right away. Ji-Eun eventually became so sleep deprived that she quit her job and now works as a freelancer from home. She also got help from the Dream Sleep Clinic in Gangnam. The business of helping millions of sleep-deprived Koreans has now grown into a $3 billion industry.

● **For Further Discussion:**

1. According to the BBC, "South Korea is one of the most sleep-deprived nations on Earth." Do you agree with this statement? What dangers does lack of sleep pose for Korean society?
2. How much sleep do you usually get each night? Do you think it's enough? What would you have to change about your lifestyle to get more sleep?

— What happened?
— He hit my car and went under my car.
— Have you been drinking? You smell like alcohol.
— I have no idea.
— What do you mean?
— I'm too drunk as a skunk to remember it.
— I'm arresting you for DUI.

I hope he doesn't ask me about it. Actually, I was walking while intoxicated myself.

Topic Preview:

In your country, what are the steps that a person must take to get a driver's license? Who is the safest driver that you know? Who is the worst driver that you know? Have you ever ridden in a car with a bad driver? What happened?

Dialogue:

Barbara: Hey, Michael. Can you do me a favor?

Michael: Well, that depends on what kind of favor. What do you need?

Barbara: Could you give me a ride to the Atlanta airport next Friday morning?

Michael: What time exactly?

Barbara: Well, my flight leaves at 10:00 am, so I'd like to be there by 8:00.

Michael: I see. Well, I think I can handle that, but we'll have to leave by 7:00 am.

Barbara: Okay. That's fine. By the way, are you a safe driver?

Michael: Of course! I've been driving since I was 16 years old, and I've never had an accident.

Barbara: Well, you're only 20 years old now, so that's only four years of driving experience.

Michael: True, but I've never had an accident, and I certainly don't drink and drive.

Barbara: Okay. Well, I really appreciate your help. I'll see you at 7:00 am on Friday. Oh, I'll also give you $20 to help pay for gas.

Michael: That sounds good. All contributions are appreciated!

Traffic Accidents

On October 3, 2018, 18-year-old Kim Seon-woong was headed home around 3:00 am from his part-time job in Jeju City. When Kim noticed an elderly lady struggling to pull a handcart across the street, he decided to become a Good Samaritan and began to help her. Suddenly, a large truck appeared, barreling down the narrow street in excess of 50 kmh. The vehicle struck Kim, critically injuring him. The woman was unharmed. Kim was rushed to the hospital, but four days later, when it was obvious that he was brain dead, his father donated Kim's organs, which enhanced the lives and health of seven other people. Shockingly, the Korean media referred to the incident as an "unexpected accident." One international observer, Sam Macdonald, stated, "The idea that the resulting death was unforeseeable, or an unpreventable accident, is absurd."

The case of Kim Seon-woong illustrates a sad reality about life in Korea: it is often dangerous to cross the street. In early 2021, a sixth grader, who was crossing the street in a residential area in Seoul, was run down and killed by an SUV. In Incheon, a young mother and her 4-year-old daughter were also simply trying to cross the street in a pedestrian crosswalk. They were on their way to the girl's kindergarten when the mother was struck by a car and dragged five meters. She later died of her injuries. These hapless individuals represent just a few of the more than 3,000 Koreans who are killed every year because of traffic accidents.

For years, Korea has had one of the highest rates of deaths due to traffic accidents among OECD members. However, in mid-2022, Koreans finally received some good news. Traffic accidents dropped to their lowest level since 1970. However, fatalities involving two-wheeled vehicles and bicycles increased.

ISSUE 27 TRAFFIC ACCIDENTS

Vocabulary & Expressions:

Good Samaritan — *a person who helps others who are experiencing difficult situations
- Jesus told the story of the **Good Samaritan** (Luke 10:30-37) to answer the question "Who is my neighbor?"

barrel — *to move at a high speed
- The driver was **barreling** down the street and could not stop when the traffic light turned red.

critically — *relating to a serious injury, illness, or condition that could lead to death
- The actor was **critically** injured after crashing his car into a tree.

enhance — *to make better; to increase or improve in value or quality
- Daily exercise is one of the best ways to **enhance** your physical and mental health.

unforeseeable — *describing an event or problem you could not see or know about beforehand
- Earthquakes are **unforeseeable** events; they can happen at any time.

unpreventable — *unavoidable, inescapable, inevitable
- Some diseases are **unpreventable**, but others are preventable if you take good care of your health.

absurd — *totally unreasonable, untrue, or foolish; ridiculous
- The judge described the drunk driver's excuses as **absurd**.

run down — *to hit someone with a car, especially due to careless driving
- The drunk driver drove on the sidewalk and almost **ran down** an entire family.

SUV — *sport utility vehicle; a type of car that combines features of normal passenger cars with features of off-road vehicles, such as four-wheel drive
- The Kia Sportage is one of the most popular **SUVs** in the USA.

pedestrian — *a person who is walking
- Drivers must watch carefully for **pedestrians** crossing the street.

hapless — *unfortunate, unlucky
- The **hapless** runner fell down at the start of the race.

fatality — *a death resulting from a disaster or accident
- The word *casualty* refers to an injury, illness, or death caused by an accident, but the word *fatality* is only used to refer to a death.

Open to Debate (1): 30 Korean Issues

Discussion Points:

1. Why does Korea have such a high rate of traffic accidents? Is it because they are always in a hurry?
2. What are the most common types of bad driving behavior that you have seen?
3. How can Korea reduce its level of traffic accidents?
4. Have you ever been involved in or witnessed a traffic accident? What happened?

Read the following quotes about driving.
Can you explain what they mean? Do you agree with the idea expressed?

5. Chance takers are accident makers. Unknown
6. Drive as if every child on the street were your own. Unknown
7. Have you ever noticed that anybody driving slower than you is an idiot, and anyone going faster than you is crazy? George Carlin
8. Don't learn safety by accident. Unknown

Current Hot Topic: The Yoon Chang-ho Law

In 2018, a man named Park made a fateful decision. Even though he had consumed a lot of alcohol, he got into his BMW and started driving. Yoon Chang-ho, a 22-year-old student, and his friend were waiting at a crosswalk, when the drunken Mr. Park suddenly drove his car into them. Yoon fell into a coma and died in the hospital 46 days later, while his friend was severely injured. Park was arrested and sentenced to six years in prison. Because of public anger about the incident, lawmakers passed the "Yoon Chang-ho Law," which increased the punishment for drunk drivers.

For Further Discussion:

1. Do you think the six-year prison sentence for Park was adequate? How much prison time should he have received?
2. The Yoon Chang-ho Law reduced the blood alcohol content for drunk driving from 0.05% to 0.03%. Do you think that's a reasonable change? What penalty should a driver receive for drunk driving? Would you ever ride in a car with a friend who has been drinking?

Facebook and Twitter provide new episodes every ten seconds. People don't need me anymore. Now is the time for me to retire and let new players compete in the ring.

Facebook and Twitter are fighting for the championship, but they will become history sooner or later. People are forgetting their names, and I'm replacing them rapidly.

Topic Preview:

What types of TV shows do you prefer to watch: dramas, comedies, game shows, or something else? Is there any genre of TV show that you don't like? What are your favorite foreign TV shows? Do you ever watch any Korean "eating shows" (*mukbang*)? Why have these shows become so popular?

Dialogue:

Robert: Ashley, have you seen any good TV dramas lately? I just finished watching *The Rings of Power*, and I'm looking for a new drama to watch.

Ashley: Have you seen any Korean TV dramas? They're very popular nowadays.

Robert: No, I haven't seen any of them. What do you recommend?

Ashley: Well, the first one that I watched was called *Kingdom*. It takes place during 16th century Korea and combines political thriller with zombie horror.

Robert: Zombies? In ancient Korea? You must be kidding!

Ashley: No, not at all. I don't normally like zombie shows, but this one is really good. The scenery, costumes, and sets are just outstanding. It also stars Ju Ji-hoon and Bae Doo-na, two of my favorite Korean actors.

Robert: Well, I don't know if I would like it. It doesn't sound like my cup of tea.

Ashley: That's exactly what I thought until I watched it. You should watch the first episode and see if you like it.

Robert: Okay. Based on your recommendation, I will watch the first episode.

Ashley: After that, you might want to see *Squid Game, Itaewon Class, Beyond Evil, Crash Landing on You, Stranger, Mr. Sunshine, Jirisan, The Good Detective, Law School*…

Robert: Hold on! I can't remember all of those!

Ashley: Okay. I'll make a list and give it to you later.

TV Dramas

Seong Gi-hun is truly down on his luck. For starters, he is divorced and estranged from his daughter and ex-wife. He also has a gambling addiction, which is impossible to support with his meager salary as a chauffeur. He has accumulated huge debts with loan sharks. He lives with his elderly mother to save money and to show that he is financially stable enough to gain custody of his daughter, Ga-yeong. In fact, she is planning to leave Korea for the United States very soon with her mother and stepfather.

Seong believes he can hit it big on the next horse racing event, so he steals some money from his mother. He places a bet, which turns out to be a big winner. He cashes in his ticket and happily begins to leave the area with his $4,000. Unfortunately, he gets another bad break. A pickpocket bumps into him and steals his money. Now he is in worse shape than before. When a stranger suddenly gives him a chance to earn a huge amount of money in a deadly competition, he readily accepts. What will become of Seong?

Seong Gi-hun is not a real person. He is a fictional character in *Squid Game*, a Korean TV drama that reached number one in 94 countries. Hwang Dong-hyuk, the writer and director, described the drama as "a story about losers." He added, "I wanted to create something that would resonate not just for Korean people but globally. The overall global economic order is unequal, and around 90% of the people believe that it's unfair." Thus, Hwang identified one of the main reasons Korean TV dramas have become so popular around the world: they show the struggles that all people face. In addition, the producers develop the stories with excellent acting and production.

ISSUE 28 TV DRAMAS

Vocabulary & Expressions:

down on one's luck
*experiencing bad luck, especially financial difficulties
- Ever since my uncle quit his job, he's been **down on his luck**.

for starters
*to begin with
- I cannot attend the concert; **for starters**, the tickets are too expensive.

estranged
*no longer friendly; not speaking
- My cousins have been **estranged** ever since they had a bad argument.

meager
*not enough in amount or quality
- The minimum wage of $7.25/hour is too **meager** to support a family.

chauffeur
*a person hired to drive people around in a car; a paid driver
- Rich people often hire a **chauffeur** to drive their children to school.

loan shark
*a person who lends money to individuals at very high rates of interest
- **Loan sharks** make illegal loans and use threats of violence to collect their money.

stable
*describing a reliable situation that is not likely to change
- Before you get married, you should save enough money to be financially **stable**.

custody
*direct responsibility for the care and control of someone
- In the case of divorce, mothers often get **custody** of the children.

hit it big
*to find great success
- Arnold Schwarzenegger **hit it big** in Hollywood when he appeared in *Conan the Barbarian* (1982).

bad break
*a situation of bad luck; opposite of *lucky break*
- My favorite team was ready for the big game, but unfortunately, they got a **bad break**: two players got sick.

pickpocket
*a thief who skillfully steals from pockets and purses
- Tourists who visit Barcelona, Rome, or Paris have to watch carefully for **pickpockets**.

resonate
*to produce a positive feeling, opinion, or emotional response
- The president's proposal to lower taxes clearly **resonated** with voters.

●●●● *Open to Debate (1): 30 Korean Issues*

● **Discussion Points:**

1. Why do you think Korean TV dramas have become so popular around the world?
2. What is your opinion of the drama *Squid Game*? What are your favorite Korean TV dramas?
3. If you were in dire financial straits, would you participate in a competition like that in *Squid Game*? If not, how would you free yourself from financial difficulties?
4. In *Squid Game*, participants play six children's games: red light, green light; sugar honeycombs (*dalgona*); tug of war; marbles; hopscotch; and squid game. Have you ever played any of these games? Which were your favorites?

Read the following quotes taken from Korean TV dramas.
Can you explain what they mean? Do you agree with the idea expressed?

5. There's an Indian proverb that goes, "Sometimes, the wrong train takes you to the right station." *Crash Landing on You* (2019–20), starring Hyun Bin and Son Ye-jin
6. At the end of the day, there is only one thing that never changes: the fact that nothing is forever. *Now, We Are Breaking Up* (2021–22), starring Song Hye-kyo and Jang Ki-yong
7. Do you know what someone with no money has in common with someone with too much money? Living is no fun for them. *Squid Game* (2021–22), starring Lee Jung-jae and Park Hae-soo

● **Current Hot Topic: Korean Dramas and Korean Food**

Korean dramas have not only spread Korean culture and creativity around the world, they have also introduced traditional Korean foods to an international audience. *Itaewon Class* (2020) is a case in point. In this award-winning drama, Park Sae-ro-yi (Park Seo-joon) is the owner of a bar-restaurant called DanBam. His ultimate goal is to expand his business into a franchise and defeat his rival, the CEO of Jangga Group. Through this outstanding drama, global viewers are left hungering for many delightful Korean foods, including kimchi fried rice, ramyun, *jajangmyeon*, *kimbap*, *chimaek*, *samgyeopsal*, *omurice*, *kongnamul guk*, *sundubu-jjigae*, *jamppong*, *jeyuk-bokkeum*, and many more.

● **For Further Discussion:**

1. Why do producers of Korean TV dramas choose to include food in so many scenes? What can people learn about Korean culture from watching scenes related to food?
2. What Korean foods are your favorites? Are there any Korean foods that you don't like? How many of the foods listed above can you cook?

> **IS A COLLEGE EDUCATION WORTH YOUR TIME AND MONEY?**
> 1. Who's going to ask a painter to see a diploma? They would say, "Can I see your paintings?" wouldn't they?
> 2. If you think education is expensive, try ignorance.

Some say a college education is useless while others say it's worth the investment. I have no choice but to go to college to know who is right.

I agree that a college education is getting too expensive these days, and graduates suffer from huge debts after finishing school. I'm going to try ignorance and see what will happen.

Topic Preview:

When you were in high school, did your parents ever monitor your schoolwork to make sure you were getting good grades? Did they ever tell you that it's very important that you go to college? What reasons did they give? Considering the fact that it's difficult to find a job nowadays, do you think a college diploma is still worth the time and money involved?

Dialogue:

Amanda: Hi, William! I haven't seen you for a while. What have you been up to?

William: Hi, Amanda. Well, I just graduated from college two months ago, and now I'm looking for a job.

Amanda: Well, congratulations! How's the job search going?

William: Not too well at the moment. I'm starting to think that I made a mistake by majoring in liberal arts.

Amanda: Oh, that's too bad. What kind of job are you looking for?

William: I was hoping to get a job in public relations or as an editor for a publication.

Amanda: And there aren't many jobs in those fields?

William: That's it exactly. At the moment, I'm just working a part-time job at Starbucks.

Amanda: Well, at least you are earning some money.

William: Yeah, it's better than nothing, but pretty soon, I have to start paying on my student loans.

Amanda: Well, I wish you good luck. I'll be looking for a job myself in a year or so.

Value of a College Education

It is an understatement to say that education is important in South Korea. Education is truly the highest priority for most families. Parents constantly stress to their children the view that education is crucial for upward mobility in Korean society. Children are ingrained with the belief that they must succeed in school and in college in order to get a prestigious white-collar job. Also, this accomplishment will uphold the family honor, and as an added benefit, if young people attend the best college, they will also gain access to a better pool of potential marriage partners. As a result of the emphasis on education, more than 80% of Korean students go to college, and Korea has one of the world's most highly educated labor forces.

With such a well-educated workforce, college graduates in Korea experience intense competition when they try to get employment at a top-tier company. In a recent survey, almost two-thirds of college seniors and graduates said that they have given up looking for work. Only one in ten respondents is actively looking for a job. Most of them feel disillusioned and depressed. This fact helps explain why the number of Koreans seeking treatment for mood disorders has topped one million. Almost 20% of them are people in their 20s, and the number of those in their 20s exceeds those in their 60s.

To compound their problems, many college graduates only think about working for a conglomerate. They refuse to consider taking a less prestigious job at a small or midsize company. To make matters worse, the COVID-19 pandemic decreased the number of job openings. In response to a dwindling supply of jobs, many graduates are returning to college to study for higher degrees. Others are preparing to take exams that would qualify them for civil service jobs.

ISSUE 29 VALUE OF A COLLEGE EDUCATION

Vocabulary & Expressions:

understatement — *a statement that makes something seem smaller or less important than it really is
- To say that Warren Buffet is "a good businessman" is an ***understatement***; he's a multibillionaire!

upward mobility — *having the opportunity and ability to rise to a higher economic or social position
- Graduating from an Ivy League school, like Harvard or Yale, automatically gives you a lot of ***upward mobility***.

ingrained — *firmly fixed; deep-rooted; deeply impressed
- In Asia, respect for elders is ***ingrained*** in children from an early age.

white-collar — *relating to workers whose work does not involve physical labor or wearing work clothes
- ***White-collar*** jobs usually have higher salaries, but ***blue-collar*** workers, like plumbers and electricians, also make a good salary.

intense — *very great in degree; of extreme force, strength, or amount
- There was an ***intense*** struggle between West Germany and Argentina during the 1990 World Cup final, but West Germany finally won by a score of 2-1.

disillusioned — *having lost faith or trust in something that you previously thought was good or valuable
- The older I get, the more ***disillusioned*** I become with politics.

mood disorder — *a mental condition characterized by abnormal feelings and attitudes
- ***Mood disorders***, such as depression, are often stress related.

compound — *to make worse; to add to
- The soccer player hurt his leg badly; then to ***compound*** his problems, he got COVID-19.

conglomerate — *a corporation engaging in many different kinds of businesses
- The largest ***conglomerates*** in Korea are Samsung Electronics, Hyundai Motor, and SK Holdings.

dwindling — *becoming less or smaller
- My food supply in the kitchen is ***dwindling***; I need to go shopping.

civil service — *the branch of a government that takes care of the daily business of running the government, not including the legislature, legal system, or military
- ***Civil service*** jobs include mail carrier, building inspector, tax collector, and social worker.

Open to Debate (1): 30 Korean Issues

Discussion Points:

1. Do you know any recent college graduates who are looking for a job? What is their life like?
2. What can the Korean government do to encourage young people to take jobs at small and midsize companies?
3. Every country needs many workers who are skilled in trades, such as carpenters, plumbers, electricians, and car mechanics. Would you ever consider preparing for this type of job?
4. If you cannot get a job in the future, which would you prefer: to study for a civil service job or to go back to college to study for a higher degree?

Read the following quotes about a college education.
Can you explain what they mean? Do you agree with the idea expressed?

5. Fathers send their sons to college either because they went to college or because they didn't. L. L. Henderson
6. I'm going to college. I don't care if it ruins my career. I'd rather be smart than a movie star. Natalie Portman
7. College is the reward for surviving high school. Judd Apatow

Current Hot Topic: Job Searching, Student Loans, and Depression

A recent survey of college graduates in Korea who were going through the stress of job searching revealed a shocking fact. About 40% said that they had experienced depression, but about 15% (1 out 7) reported actually being suicidal. Graduates who majored in liberal arts or social science endured more stress than those who majored in natural science or engineering. Graduates who had accumulated large student loans were among the most depressed. According to one report, just three out of ten recent college graduates are able to repay their student loans because they can only get low-paying or part-time jobs.

For Further Discussion:

1. Why do you think majors in liberal arts or social science experience more stress than majors in natural science or engineering?
2. Have you ever taken out a student loan? Did you repay it? What happens to graduates who cannot repay their student loans?

Whenever I make money, I put it in my safe. I know I can't be rich, but at least I won't lose it. But inflation is my worst enemy, so I am lobbying for deflation.

I know how to make money in the stock market. I buy stocks in a BEAR MARKET and sell them in a BULL MARKET. If you apply this strategy to your investments, you will have zero possibility of losing your money.

The most important investment you can make is IN YOURSELF.

Topic Preview:

Do you think the stock market is a good investment? Have you ever bought any stocks? What type of stocks did you buy? What cryptocurrencies are popular where you live (e.g., Bitcoin, Ethereum, Dogecoin)? Do you know anyone who invested money in cryptocurrency? What happened?

Dialogue:

James: Mary, do you ever invest in the stock market?

Mary: Yes, I do, but I only buy blue chip stocks, like Coca-Cola, Walmart, and Nike.

James: Well, I just came across a stock that I think would be a good investment.

Mary: Yeah, what's that?

James: It's a company called Hello Pal International. It's going to be the next Facebook. Right now, it's available at only $0.09 per share. It's supposed to go up to $1.19 per share within a year.

Mary: You must be kidding! That's a penny stock. Most people who invest in those stocks lose their shirt.

James: Well, not everyone. When Apple Inc. was first offered, one share cost less than $1.00. Now, it's worth almost $400 per share.

Mary: That may be true, but there are thousands of penny stocks. Picking one that will be as successful as Apple is almost impossible.

James: Well, I'd like to try.

Mary: Okay, but remember the old proverb that says, "Don't put all your eggs in one basket." Just invest a small amount in penny stocks.

James: Okay. I will follow your advice.

ISSUE-30

126 Open to Debate (1): *30 Korean Issues*

Where to Invest

Koreans have long been known as great savers. Studies show that 97% of Koreans save money. Among OECD members, with respect to personal savings, Koreans are second only to Poland. However, like most people, Koreans are in a quandary about the best place to invest their money. If you put your money into a certificate of deposit, you can count yourself lucky if you get 3% annual interest. At that rate, if you invest $1,000 and wait patiently for a year, you will only have $1,030. Due to inflation, your total savings may have less value than when you made your first deposit.

Because of the eroding value of money over time, many Koreans are investing in the stock market. A recent survey asked Koreans in their 20s and 30s how they are investing their money. Almost 90% of them answered that they are buying stocks. About 28% of respondents said that they invested less than 10% of their monthly income. However, about 11% were investing aggressively and putting more than half of their monthly income into stocks and other investments. When asked about their actual profits, the answers showed how risky stock investments really are: 52% said they had made a profit, while the other 48% confessed that they had broken even or lost money.

Many young investors buy stocks in order to save up enough money to buy a home. This aim is certainly a worthy goal because one of the best investments that anyone can make is to buy real estate. Unfortunately, due to soaring housing prices, it is impossible for young people to buy a home just by saving their money in a bank, as older generations did. Stocks are great investments if you choose wisely and avoid those that are highly speculative, especially penny stocks.

ISSUE 30 WHERE TO INVEST

Vocabulary & Expressions:

quandary
*a state of doubt or confusion
- When I saw my friend cheating on the exam, I was in a *quandary* about what to do.

certificate of deposit
*an agreement with a bank by which you deposit a sum of money for a specific length of time at a specific interest rate
- If I buy a *certificate of deposit* for one year, my bank will pay 2% interest; if I buy it for three years, they will pay 2.5% interest.

count
*to consider or believe to be
- *Count* yourself lucky if you don't get COVID-19.

deposit
*money that is put into a bank account; opposite of *withdrawal*
- My parents make a *deposit* of $20 into my bank account every week.

eroding
*decreasing, weakening, diminishing
- European leaders are concerned about the *eroding* value of the euro.

aggressively
*describing an investment approach that takes some risks to get better returns on investment
- It's unwise to invest *aggressively* if you don't have much money.

confess
*to admit that something is true, especially if it's embarrassing
- I *confessed* to my teacher that I had not read the book.

break even
*to operate a business or make an investment without losing money or making money
- My uncle's new bakery only *broke even* the first year; after that, he started making a profit.

worthy
*having value or excellence
- Helping the poor is a *worthy* goal for any citizen.

soar
*to increase quickly
- Fuel prices began to *soar* after the war started.

speculative
*involving a big risk in investments in hopes of making a big profit
- Investing in cryptocurrency is highly *speculative*.

penny stock
*a very risky stock usually selling for less than a dollar
- Monster Beverage was once a *penny stock*, selling for $0.50 per share; now it sells for more than $52 per share.

Open to Debate (1): 30 Korean Issues

Open to Debate (1): 30 Korean Issues

● Discussion Points:

1. Why do so many people lose money investing in the stock market?
2. If you had $10,000 to invest in the stock market, would you buy "blue chips" (stocks of old, trustworthy companies) or stocks of new companies?
3. Do you have the goal of buying a home? When do you think you'll be able to buy it?
4. Did your parents teach you to save money? How did they motivate you to save money?

Read the following quotes about investing.
Can you explain what they mean? Do you agree with the idea expressed?

5. Risk comes from not knowing what you're doing. Warren Buffett
6. Price is what you pay. Value is what you get. Warren Buffett
7. Be fearful when others are greedy and greedy when others are fearful. Warren Buffett
8. An investment in knowledge pays the best interest. Benjamin Franklin
9. How many millionaires do you know who have become wealthy by investing in savings accounts? Unknown
10. The biggest risk of all is not taking one. Mellody Hobson

● **Current Hot Topic: Bitcoin: A Smart Investment?**

In 2010, the highest price Bitcoin reached was only $0.39. Over the next decade, the price was extremely volatile but reached a peak of $63,558 on April 12, 2021. However, in early 2022, Bitcoin's price steadily declined, and by March, it was well below $50,000. Among the many Koreans who thought it was the perfect time to buy Bitcoin was a certain Mr. Lee. He invested heavily in Bitcoin and even borrowed money to buy more, all without informing his wife, who was pregnant. When the price plummeted, leaving Lee with huge debts, his angry wife demanded a divorce.

● **For Further Discussion:**

1. Do you own any Bitcoin or other cryptocurrency? Would you like to buy some? Which cryptocurrency do you think is the best investment?
2. Read the following quotes about Bitcoin. Do you agree with the idea expressed?
   - Bitcoin will do to banks what email did to the postal industry. Rick Falkvinge
   - Bitcoin is the most important invention in the history of the world since the Internet. Roger Ver

Notes about Grammar and Style

The purpose of this appendix is to make a few observations about grammar and style that users of this book may find helpful.

1. American English

There are many varieties of English in use in the world, but the two that are found most often are American English and British English. It is best to view these as two models for learning English. In many parts of the world, British English is the preferred model; in other areas, American English is preferred. It is best to choose one model and stick with it. In this book, we follow the American English model.

2. Abbreviations

We use few abbreviations in this book, but it will be helpful to list them here.

AKA	also known as
e.g.	*exempli gratia*, a Latin expression that means "for example." This expression is used when you want to cite an example of something.
etc.	*et cetera*, a Latin expression that means "and the rest." In modern usage, etc. means "and so on" or "and so forth." This expression is used at the end of a list to show that other things could be added to the list.
i.e.	*id est*, a Latin expression meaning "that is" or "in other words."

3. Styles of Writing

When writing in English, how do you know when to use a comma, hyphen, and other marks of punctuation? To answer specific questions about punctuation, spelling, use of numbers, and other matters of style, it is best to choose a style guide to follow. If you are taking an English writing class, your teacher may ask you to follow a specific guide. Four main styles exist in modern English writing.

AP	*Associated Press Stylebook*	Newspaper style
APA	*Publication Manual of the American Psychological Association*	Science style
CMOS	*The Chicago Manual of Style*	Book-editing style
MLA	*MLA Handbook* [Modern Language Association of America]	Academic style

In this book, we mostly follow the *CMOS* style.

One of the unique aspects of *CMOS* style lies in the way it uses hyphens. In many cases, a hyphen is used in a compound adjective when it appears before a noun, but not when it occurs after a noun. Thus, the hyphen is omitted in the second example below, even though dictionaries show the word *well-known* with a hyphen.

> John is a *well-known* teacher.
> John is *well known* in the community.

If you would like to learn the *CMOS* rules about using hyphens, just google "*CMOS* hyphen style guide," and you will be able to find a chart showing all the *CMOS* rules.

4. Spelling

Many English words have alternate spellings. For example, which of the following words is spelled correctly: *lifestyle*, *life style*, *life-style*? If you consult Dictionary.com, you will see all three spellings listed as possibilities, though *lifestyle* is the first one listed. If you consult Merriam-Webster.com, you find only the spelling *lifestyle*. Likewise, which is the correct spelling: *smartphone* or *smart phone*? Both are possible, but *smartphone* is the preferred spelling according to Merriam-Webster. For matters of spelling in this book, we follow Merriam-Webster.com

5. Gender Neutrality

Before the 1970s, writers often used the pronouns *he/him/his* in a generic sense to represent both genders. It was common to read sentences like this:

> If a student wants to get an A+, *he* must turn in all *his* homework on time.

In this sentence, *he* represents *he or she*, and *his* represents *his or her*. However, many writers object to this generic use of *he* to represent both genders as a sexist practice. Therefore, since the 1970s, writers have used various techniques to avoid such gender-biased language.

APPENDIX

In this book, we use a variety of methods to express gender. In some cases, we use *he/his/him* in a generic sense to refer to either gender:

Would you vote for a politician in *his* 70s or 80s?

In other cases, we use *she/her* in a generic sense to refer to either gender:

If a teacher is kind, *her* students will experience bonding with *her*.

Sometimes, we use *he or she*:

Do you think *he or she* [a highly paid CEO] is worth that much money?

We also use modern gender-neutral words for occupations instead of old-fashioned, gender-biased words. The words in the first column below are preferred.

fisher	fisherman
firefighter	fireman
police officer	policeman
server	waiter/waitress
host	host/hostess

We use *they/them/their* where the gender of a person could be male or female.

When a driver is using the autopilot feature, *they* must still pay attention to driving.

Do you know anyone who is a vegetarian? What are *their* reasons for choosing that lifestyle?

Some writers object to the use of *they* to represent *he/she* and *their* to represent *his/her*. However, Michael Swan points out:

This use of *they/them/their* has existed for centuries and is perfectly correct. It is most common in an informal style, but can also be found in formal written English (*Practical English Usage*, 3rd ed. Oxford University Press, 2005, p. 521).

6. Capitalization of Black

In 2020, the Associated Press announced that it was making a major change in the *AP Stylebook*. Going forward, the news organization would capitalize the "b" in the word *Black* when the word was used to refer to people in a racial, ethnic, or cultural context.

APPENDIX

A spokesperson for the AP said that the change was intended to convey a shared sense of history and identity that exists among Black people. He added, "The lowercase *black* is a color, not a person."

In addition to capitalizing the word Black when referring to *Black* people, the *AP* said that it would also capitalize the word *Indigenous* when it was used to refer to the original inhabitants of a place. However, the *AP* stated that it would not capitalize the word *brown*, which has sometimes been used to refer to Latinos. The *AP* added that writers should avoid using the word *brown* to refer to people, describing the word as a broad and imprecise term for the purpose of making racial, ethnic, or cultural references.

The *AP Stylebook*'s new policy also stated that the word *white* should not be capitalized when referring to white people. The *AP* pointed out that white people have less of a shared history and culture than Black people, and white people don't generally have the experience of being discriminated against because of skin color.

Following the changes in the *AP Stylebook*, numerous news organizations have also changed their style guides to capitalize *Black*, including the *Los Angeles Times*, *Boston Globe*, *Seattle Times*, and *USA Today*. The *CMOS* also announced that they now recommend capitalizing *Black* when it refers to people in a racial or ethnic sense.

Other news organizations, such as CNN and Fox News, announced that they would also capitalize the word *white* when it referred to white people as a racial group. They explained that capitalizing *white* was consistent with the capitalization of Black, Asian, Latino, and other ethnic groups.

In this book, we capitalize *Black* and *Indigenous* when referring to people as a racial group. However, we do not capitalize *white* and *brown*.

What's Inside

Open to Debate 2 — 30 Global Issues

Issue 01	Access to Education
Issue 02	Artificial Intelligence
Issue 03	Child Labor and Trafficking
Issue 04	Child Marriage
Issue 05	Climate Change
Issue 06	Corruption
Issue 07	COVID-19
Issue 08	Digital Currencies
Issue 09	Drug Abuse
Issue 10	Euthanasia
Issue 11	Factory Farming
Issue 12	Gender Equality
Issue 13	Great Power Conflicts
Issue 14	Human Trafficking
Issue 15	Hunger and Malnourishment
Issue 16	Immigration
Issue 17	Internet Addiction
Issue 18	Internet Censorship
Issue 19	LGBTQ
Issue 20	Life Expectancy
Issue 21	Natural Disasters
Issue 22	Obesity
Issue 23	Pollution
Issue 24	Population Growth
Issue 25	Same-Sex Marriage
Issue 26	Smoking in Developing Countries
Issue 27	Social Media
Issue 28	Suicide
Issue 29	Surveillance and Privacy
Issue 30	Terrorism

Open to Debate 3 — 30 Money Issues

Issue 01	A Country Goes Bankrupt?
Issue 02	A Delivery War among Supermarkets
Issue 03	Aging Populations
Issue 04	American Greed
Issue 05	Bitcoin
Issue 06	Credit Card Debt
Issue 07	Cybersecurity and Your Money
Issue 08	Dog Day Care
Issue 09	Drinking and Productivity
Issue 10	Educated but Unemployed
Issue 11	Excessive Compensation for CEOs
Issue 12	Future Energy
Issue 13	Global Trade Protectionism
Issue 14	Governmental Control of Obesity
Issue 15	Home Ownership
Issue 16	Internet Millionaire
Issue 17	Jobs of the Future
Issue 18	Labor Unions
Issue 19	Leaving Money to Your Children
Issue 20	Loaning Money to Family and Friends
Issue 21	Money and Happiness
Issue 22	National Pension Plans
Issue 23	Sexual Harassment in the Workplace
Issue 24	Student Loans and Student Debt
Issue 25	The Business of Corruption
Issue 26	The Frenzy of Black Friday
Issue 27	The Lottery
Issue 28	The Power of Inflation
Issue 29	The World's Most Expensive Health Care
Issue 30	Wealth Inequality

Open to Debate 4 30 Cultural Issues

Issue 01	Alcohol
Issue 02	Babysitting
Issue 03	Breastfeeding
Issue 04	Bribery
Issue 05	Cell Phones
Issue 06	Clothing
Issue 07	Cost of Health Care
Issue 08	Crime and Punishment
Issue 09	Dating
Issue 10	Driving
Issue 11	Funerals and Burial
Issue 12	Gender Roles
Issue 13	Gestures and Body Language
Issue 14	LGBTQ Rights
Issue 15	Marriage and Divorce
Issue 16	Obesity
Issue 17	Personal Space
Issue 18	Public Display of Affection
Issue 19	Public Nudity
Issue 20	Racism
Issue 21	Retirement
Issue 22	Shopping
Issue 23	Smoking Bans
Issue 24	Strange Laws
Issue 25	Superstitions
Issue 26	Time and Punctuality
Issue 27	Tipping
Issue 28	Toilets
Issue 29	Weddings
Issue 30	Work and Vacations

Open to Debate 5 30 American Issues

Issue 01	Abortion
Issue 02	Age Discrimination
Issue 03	Anti-Vaxxers
Issue 04	Black Lives Matter
Issue 05	Breastfeeding in Public
Issue 06	CEO Salaries
Issue 07	College Admissions
Issue 08	Death Penalty
Issue 09	Drug Dependence
Issue 10	DUI
Issue 11	Equal Justice
Issue 12	FBI Surveillance
Issue 13	Fraud
Issue 14	Gender Diversity
Issue 15	Gun Violence
Issue 16	Health Care
Issue 17	Hot Car Death
Issue 18	Immigration
Issue 19	Police Brutality
Issue 20	Poverty
Issue 21	Racially Motivated Violence
Issue 22	Rich Pastors
Issue 23	Risky Activities
Issue 24	Road Rage
Issue 25	Same-Sex Marriage
Issue 26	Service Dogs
Issue 27	Student Loans
Issue 28	Transgender People
Issue 29	Universal Basic Income
Issue 30	White Supremacy

DISCUSSION TEXTBOOK
FROM LIS KOREA

중고급 어린이들을 위한 독창적인 영어교재

New Children's Talk (1), (2), (3)

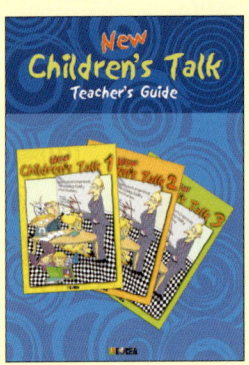

교사용

New Children's Talk (TG)

- 일상생활에서 벌어지는 상황들을 다양한 포맷에 맞추어서 많은 Speaking Chance를 제공합니다.
- 암기 위주의 영어가 아니라 자기 의견을 만들어 낼 수 있는 포맷들을 제공합니다.

청소년의 세계와 그들의 생각 관심사들을 토론으로

Chat Room for Teens (1), (2), (3)

- New Children's Talk를 배운 학생들이 Teen Talk를 쉽게 익힐 수 있는 선행학습교재로 사용할 수 있도록 구성
- 학습의 재미와 능률을 높이기 위해 다양한 그림들과 그것들을 바탕으로 한 토론들 그리고 실제 많은 상황에서 발생하는 대화들과 수많은 지문들을 바탕으로 토론의 다양성을 확보

DISCUSSION TEXTBOOK
FROM LIS KOREA

토론교재의 베스트셀러

교사용

Debate Club for Teens (1), (2), (3) / TG

- 청소년들이 체계적으로 토론 영어를 학습할 수 있는 중·고급 교재입니다.
- 1권에서는 논리적 토론에 필요한 다양한 연습과정을 거치며, 2권에서는 제시된 다양한 주제에 대해 실전 토론을 거쳐 3권에서는 심화 주제에 대한 논리적 토론을 완성하게 됩니다.
- 청소년들의 모든 생각과 상상력을 영어로 토론할 수 있는 최상의 교재입니다.

자유 토론을 위한 훈련교재

3rd Edition All New
Talk Talk Talk (1)

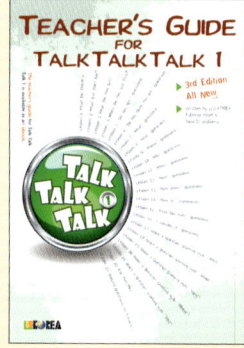

교사용

(TG)

- 새로 나온 Talk Talk Talk (1)은 전판과 비교하여, 책의 내용과 구성이 충실해졌고, 특히 각 샘플 문장마다 관련된 그림과 스토리를 더해 독자들의 흥미를 이끌어 내기 위해 많은 노력을 기울였습니다. 우리 편집진들은 400 여개의 그림과 스토리들을 통해 세상의 모든 이야기를 담으려고 했으며, 영어로 전달되는 스토리는 책 속의 또다른 재미있는 영어 학습서가 되도록 심혈을 기울였습니다. 이 책의 원래 목적인 스피킹 훈련과, 또 다른 재미있는 그림과 짧은 영어 이야기를 통해, 독자들이 한 책으로 공부와 재미 두 마리의 토끼를 잡기를 희망해 봅니다. 또한 계속해서 발행 예정인 2권, 3권에도 독자 여러분의 많은 관심 부탁드립니다.

DISCUSSION TEXTBOOK
FROM LIS KOREA

중급자들을 위한 토론교재
Speak Your Mind (1), (2)

- 일상적이며 쉬운 주제들을 선정하여 간결하게 정리했음.
- 대표 주제에 대한 질문과 대답을 여론조사 형식으로 꾸며 독자들이 쉽게 주제에 접근할 수 있도록 했음.
- 모든 주제들에 찬반 의견을 달아 독자들의 다양한 의견을 접할 수 있도록 했음.

토론교재의 베스트셀러
EXPRESS YOURSELF (1), (2), (3)
3rd Edition

- 토론 영어교재의 베스트셀러 Express Yourself 1/2/3 시리즈가 새롭게 출간되었습니다. 각 권 15개의 이슈를 깊이 있게 다루고 있으며, 다양한 토론주제와 Opinion Samples를 제공하고, 연관 dialog를 첨부하여 주제에 대한 이해력을 배가 시켰습니다.
- Points to Ponder 섹션에서는 다양한 의견들이 나올 수 있는 주제를 제시하여 다양한 토론이 되도록 했습니다.
- 토론주제와 연결되는 다양한 수백 개의 그림과 더불어 캡션을 덧붙여서 미국영어의 재미와 아름다움을 느끼도록 하였습니다.

DISCUSSION TEXTBOOK
FROM LIS KOREA

설명간결한 형식의 새로운 토론교재
Express Yourself Directly (1)

- Pictures Talk 섹션에서는 큰 주제에 대한 warm-up 주제들을 선정하여 그림과 함께 제시하여 본 주제에 쉽게 접근할 수 있도록 했습니다.
- Express Yourself Directly 섹션에서는 Pictures Talk 섹션에서 다루지 않은 좀 더 깊은 주제를 선정하여 심도 있는 토론이 되도록 했습니다.
- Let's Talk Funny 섹션에서는 본 주제와 관련 있는 재미있는 이야기를 실어 가벼운 토론과 함께 긴장을 풀도록 했습니다.
- What Does It Mean?에서는 본 주제와 관련된 Food For Thought를 제공하여 학습자들이 자유롭게 토론 할 수 있도록 했으면 다양한 의견이 나올 수 있는 문구들을 제시하였습니다.
- 마지막으로 Synopsis에서는 (전체 400의 그림으로 구성) 각 그림에 대한 설명을 영어로 명쾌하게 제시하여 학습자가 주제에 대한 최종 복습을 할 수 있도록 했습니다.

본격적인 비지니스 토론 교재
Let's Talk Business
Major New Edition

15년 만에 새롭게 바뀐 Let's Talk Business -Major New Edition-의 특징은 다음과 같습니다.

- 현재 정보화 시대에 중요한 30개의 대표 이슈들을 선정했습니다.
- 각 이슈들은 Topic preview와 Warm-up Dialog에 의해 가볍게 다루어 지며, 또한 그림과 그림에 대한 가벼운 설명으로 독자들의 흥미를 이끌어 냅니다.
- 후에 각 이슈들은 전문적인 분석으로 상세하게 다루어지며, 이후 200개 이상의 질문으로 독자들의 의견을 이끌어 내게 됩니다.
- Current Hot Topic 섹션에서는 각 이슈에 대한 보충 이슈를 다루게 되며, 다시 한번 질문을 주어 독자들의 상상력을 자극합니다.

OPEN TO DEBATE (1): 30 Korean Issues

초판 1쇄 인쇄 : 2024년 11월 01일
초판 1쇄 발행 : 2024년 11월 15일
지   은   이 : Neal D. Williams
펴   낸   곳 : (도서출판) 리스코리아
펴   낸   이 : 조은예
등   록 : 남양주 제 399-2011-000003호
전   화 : (0502) 423-7947
일러스트레이터 : 김기환
편집디자인 : 이명금, 최윤경
인   쇄 : 더블비

www.liskorea.com

All rights reserved. No part of this book may be reproduced, stored in a retrieval system, or transmitted in any form or by any means, electronic, mechanical, photocopying, recording or otherwise, without the prior permission in writing of the Publisher.

— You're gaining some weight these days, aren't you?
— It's true. But I don't know why. I just enjoy my simple hobbies: eating some fast food while watching TV or playing with my smartphone on my couch.
— Don't you know your current weight is the direct result of your hobbies? Why don't you try walking? It might help you shed your weight.
— I tried it. But the problem is that I'm always hungrier after taking a walk.

I don't eat fast food or watch TV. I have no smartphone to play with and no couch to lie down on. I don't know why I'm getting fatter too. I suspect that worrying about his obesity gives me lots of stress. My vet once told me that stress is the worst enemy you face while trying to control somebody's weight. I'll start worrying about my weight instead of worrying about his body.

— Hey, this is the third time you've asked me for a date! I've already told you NO. What part of NO do you not understand? Do you want me to report you for sexual harassment?
— How can this be harassment? It's just a simple question.
— It's harassment because you are creating an uncomfortable work environment!
— Okay, okay! I'm sorry! I won't ask again. Please don't report me.
— By the way, please keep your off-color jokes to yourself. I'm not interested in hearing them.

I used to be her boss, but I was fired because she reported me for sexual harassment. Now I can't find a new job because of my criminal record. I regret harassing her when I was there.

Smartphones have replaced your camera, calendar, and your alarm clock. Furthermore, they're replacing your family because you hug them more often and spend more time with them until you get to sleep. There must be a time coming when we're going to marry smartphones. They can talk, shop, do chores, wash the dishes, and vacuum. They can easily play the role of a spouse.

I never dreamed that I would officiate such a strange wedding between a man and his smartphone. I'm afraid someday soon we'll be replaced by smartphones too.

Today I'm marrying my smartphone. She can do everything I would expect a spouse to do. What's even better, a future divorce would be very easy, and I wouldn't have to pay any alimony.

I'm so angry that he's thinking about divorce at the exact moment we're marrying! He doesn't even know that we smartphones have progressed to the point that we're able to read his mind.

— What happened?
— He hit my car and went under my car.
— Have you been drinking? You smell like alcohol.
— I have no idea.
— What do you mean?
— I'm too drunk as a skunk to remember it.
— I'm arresting you for DUI.

I hope he doesn't ask me about it. Actually, I was walking while intoxicated myself.